H.U.Y.O.E.
NON-VIOLENCE GUIDE
FOR TODAY'S YOUTH

Hold Up Your Own End

SHARON ROSE SADDLER and **FRED VMAN WATSON**

ILLUSTRATIONS BY JAQUAN WILLIAMS

The H.U.Y.O.E. Non-Violence Guide for Youth

The challenges that children face today are not new, but, when left unaddressed, can leave emotional scars that hinder a young person's true potential. Some of these hindrances include peer assault, cyber-bullying, thoughts of suicide, harassment, lack of self-esteem, rejection, anger, rage, fear, failure, gangs, and many other potentially life-changing challenges. *The H.U.Y.O.E. Non-Violence Guide for Youth* addresses these challenges that are faced by most—if not all—youth to some degree in school, at home, and in the community. Through its lessons, this guide teaches victory over violence on three levels: primary, intermediate, and high school. It is uniquely designed to reach and teach the whole child by addressing violence towards the body, soul, and spirit. Freedom, cooperation, tolerance, happiness, honesty, love, peace, humility, respect, responsibility, simplicity, and unity are values that are integrated into every lesson.

The book has a specially designed pre- and post-test that every student should take so results can be maintained, shared, and tracked from primary and intermediate grades through high school.

DEDICATION

We dedicate this book to our mothers:

Ms. Dorothy L. Wilkinson Laws

And

Ms. Mary L. Griffin Watson

You are our most phenomenal teachers and role models.

Thank you for your wisdom, your guidance, and your love.

TABLE OF CONTENTS

INTRODUCTION

"…They are endowed by their **Creator** with certain **unalienable Rights**, that among these are Life, Liberty and the pursuit of Happiness." What a powerful promise made in the Declaration of Independence! And yet, this promise is broken every day in the lives of children across this nation due to bullying, fear of failure, physical and emotional abuse, and suicide.

The mission of The H.U.Y.O.E. Non-Violence Guide for Youth is to introduce sustainable, non-violence methodologies, strategies, and techniques that can be introduced in homes, classrooms, churches, community centers, and private settings and implemented in all environments for children between the ages of four and eighteen. Successful outcomes generated through this guide have both short and long-term educational, social, emotional, physical, and financial benefits to families and communities. This Guide is cost-effective, and is easily duplicated and adapted in all learning situations.

The objective of The H.U.Y.O.E. Non-Violence Guide for Youth is to provide support systems that help children and young adults achieve victory over any form of violence upon self or others.
The goals of The H.U.Y.O.E. Non-Violence Guide for Youth are many, including to help reduce violence over a ten-year period by creating a counter-culture to dissipate the culture of violence, and to help children become life-long practitioners of non-violent thinking and behavior. Another goal of The H.U.Y.O.E. Non-Violence Guide for Youth is to increase self-esteem. Healthy self-esteem is a great component in the success of any person, regardless of age, but is especially important in the formative years of children when they are developing social awareness and relationships. Increases in self-esteem impact short- and long-term academic achievement. Self-esteem is also a decisive factor in many decisions regarding peer-pressure, relationships, and group dynamics in the lives of teens and young adults.

Finally, our goal is to help make schools, homes, and communities "Safe Places" for all children and young adults. Children will gain understanding of how to create safe environments and safe relationships with peers, family members, and each person they interact with. They will also understand that they must take an active and knowledgeable role in the development of a healthy, non-violent environment. They will learn that even at the youngest age, children are viable and valuable stake-holders in society and its future. What they learn today will determine what they will teach tomorrow.

H.U.Y.O.E. PRE- AND POST-ASSESSMENT

PRIMARY LEVEL

- ✓ This assessment is an important tool in evaluating the effectiveness of the non-violence education that is provided.
- ✓ This assessment should be completed at the beginning of the program and again at the end. This will provide comparison data.

QUESTIONS	YES	NO	I DON'T KNOW
1. Do you know and understand the definition of violence?			
2. Do you know the warning signs of violence in you or others?			
3. Have you ever been bullied or been a victim of violence or abuse?			
4. Have you witnessed violence in a public place or at school?			
5. Do you or other people think you are a bully or a violent person?			
6. Do you believe that there are situations that require violence?			
7. Do the adults around you protect you from violence or bullying?			
8. Do you know what emotional abuse is?			
9. Does walking away from or talking out of a fight show fear ?			
10. Do you know how to improve your self-esteem?			
11. If someone makes you angry enough, is violence all right?			
12. Can you protect yourself against violence without being violent?			
13. Do adults listen to you when you are angry or upset?			
14. Is using a weapon an option in handling a fight or an argument?			
15. Do you believe that you can help reduce violence around you?			

Name: _____ Date: _____

H.U.Y.O.E. PRE- AND POST ASSESSMENT

INTERMEDIATE

> ✓ This assessment is an important tool in evaluating the effectiveness of the non-violence education that is provided.
> ✓ This assessment should be completed at the beginning of the program, and again at the end. This will provide comparison data.

1. How do people around you interact with others who are not a part of your group?

2. Do you witness disrespectful behaviors in your environment? What are they?

3. Who is usually involved with the disrespectful behavior toward you or others?

4. What can you do to help resolve or prevent events that are aggressive or violent?

5. Do you ever feel unsafe at school, at home, or in your community? Why?

6. Have you ever been threatened at school? How did you handle that?

7. Have you ever threatened anyone else at school? Why?

8. What is your greatest concern about the way your friends or family treat each other?

9. How do you show respect to other people? How do people respect you?

10. How would you define bullying?

11. Do you consider bullying a crime? Should bullies be punished by schools or law enforcement?

12. Should schools be responsible for protecting their students?

13. How do you handle extreme anger or rage?

14. What technique do you use to help de-escalate a hostile situation?

15. Is it possible to get through life without physical or emotional violence?

16. What is emotional abuse? What is mental abuse?

17. How does depression or anxiety affect you, your friends, or famly?

18. How does your self-esteem affect your friendships?

19. What do you like the most about yourself? What would you like to change?

20. Do you believe that you can make a difference in the world? Why?

Name: _____ Date: _____

WHAT IS VIOLENCE?

VIOLENCE IS ANY ACT OF INTENTIONAL HARM OR DESTRUCTION UPON ONESELF OR OTHERS.

I SHARED, I CARED AWARD

AWARDED TO YOU FOR CARING AND SHARING

NAME:_____DATE:_____

CARING AND SHARING (K – 1st grade)

DRAW PICTURES OF YOU CARING ABOUT OTHERS.

Be nice to others.	Help others when you can.
Never say things to hurt others.	Never hit or push others.

Give or share with others.	Think about others' feelings.
Be a good listener.	Let others go first.

Name: _____ Date: _____

HOW TO BE CARING

(2 - 3 grades)

Write an explanation and example for each of these statements.

Treat other people the way you want to be treated.

_____

_____

_____

_____

Be courteous and polite to everyone.

_____

_____

_____

_____

Listen to what other people have to say.

_____

_____

_____

_____

Do not insult or degrade other people.

_____

_____

_____

_____

Never bully, hit, or pick on others.

_____

_____

_____

_____

Do not judge or make fun of other people. Respect their differences.

_____

_____

_____

_____

Never call other people names.

_____

_____

_____

_____

CARING AND SHARING

IS IMPORTANT

(4 – 6 grades)

WHAT YOU THINK AND FEEL IS VERY IMPORTANT.

Your thoughts and feelings are important to you and to the people around you. If you are sad or scared, it affects everything that you do and say. It is hard to be successful in anything you do if you feel bad. But people cannot know how you feel unless you tell them. That is why it is so important to express how you really feel inside.

Why should we talk about our feelings instead of waiting for someone to guess how we feel? Can we really know how people feel inside if they do not tell us?

_____

_____

Have you ever wanted to tell someone how you felt inside, but you were afraid to tell? Who did you want to share your feelings with? How did you feel not sharing your feelings?

_____

_____

Now, think of a time that you were able to share your thoughts and feelings. How did you feel to honestly share your thoughts and feelings? Why is this important?

_____

_____

_____

CARING AND SHARING

IS IMPORTANT

(INTERMEDIATE)

WHAT YOU THINK AND FEEL IS VERY IMPORTANT.

One of the greatest assets we have is the ability to communicate. Whether it is through speaking, body language, or technology, we communicate our thoughts, feelings, likes and dislikes almost every minute in the day. Communication is essential to everyone.

Have you ever wanted to tell someone how you felt, but were afraid to say? Who did you want to share your thoughts or feelings with, but could not? How did that make you feel?

_____

_____

_____

Now, think of a time that you were able to share your thoughts and feelings with others. How did it feel to honestly share your thoughts and feelings? Why is this important?

_____

_____

_____

_____

How can technological devices (cell phones, emails, computers, video cameras, video phones, etc.) complicate or hinder our ability to truly communication with and understand other people?

_____

_____

_____

Have you ever had a misunderstanding with someone because you were not able to communicate well with them? What happened?

_____

_____

_____

_____

Was the problem resolved? How did you resolve the communication problem?

_____

_____

_____

_____

What do you feel is the best way to share your feelings with someone you care about? Why?

_____

_____

_____

_____

THE STORY OF THE LIL VMAN

AND THE V-CREW

LIL VMAN

Lil VMan is known in the World of Kids as a great hero. He battles with the makers of negative energy and hardship who work from the top of the world and sometimes from their underground headquarters.

When negativity occurs, everyone must work together to help. Lil VMan realized long ago that **one person can do a little good, but when others join that one person, they can do a lot of good together**.

Lil VMan established relationships with three others who became his VCrew: B-Girl, G-Man, and Shuk-V, a hip hop duck. They all lived near each other and wanted to help make good changes in their world.

Lil VMan's crew joined forces at a time when world was faced with extinction. Those who produced the negative energy had launched a world-wide conspiracy to have the skies all over the world fall upon mankind! If this plan were successful, it would destroy all life and positive energy upon the earth.

The plan was a big secret. Nobody saw it coming. Representatives of all of the negative energies from around the world had come together for a great meeting. When the role was called, hate, anger and rage were there; hopelessness, lack of forgiveness, pain, and fear had shown up; prejudice, denial, and depression stood waiting; apathy and abuse raised their hands; and a host of others who represent the most violent acts against mankind were in attendance at this great meeting of negative spirit and mind. These allies were all masters of deception and were governed by ignorance and inhumanity.

The agenda was simple: to produce and disburse the most destructive products they could and to make them so plentiful that the very sky would fall. Two of their most popular products that they wanted to use to cover the world were called "Be Bad" and "Make Excuses". The strategy was to do it quietly and secretly and release it upon mankind while mankind was too busy to SHARE and CARE for each other.

Meanwhile, the V-Crew was busy doing other things. Shuk-V, for example, was busy blending sounds of all animals, beast, insect and fowl, to create a new music that would become a language of peace that all animal-kind could understand and use to communicate with each other, whether they were from farm or jungle. Every animal knew of Shuk-V's dedication to music and desire to help everyone communicate with one another. The other animals respected him for it, though they did little themselves to help others.

B-GIRL

G-MAN

One day as B-Girl was flying over a great mountain which had huge caves lodged near its tops, she overheard what seemed to be an argument mixed with cheering. She slowed to gliding and began to circle, using her inner radar to hear what was going on. Little did she know that she had discovered the research and development lab for the negative energy representatives.

That is when she overheard their evil plan. She became so frightened that she nearly stopped moving her wings and crashed to earth, but she regained her composure and began to fly frantically to tell someone that the sky was going to fall, not knowing where to start. She had to find someone to talk to.

As she was flying, looking around and trying to figure out what to do, G-man raised his long neck and she flew into him.

G-Man bent his neck downward to cushion B-Girl's fall, enabling her to fall softly upon a nearby bush. When she recovered she thanked him, and then began telling him about the plan to have the sky fall. He was greatly shaken by this information, because if it were to happen, he would be among the first to feel the impact of such a terrible act since he was so very tall.

B-Girl and G-Man formed an immediate **COLLABORATION**. They began to use **CREATIVE-BRAINSTORMING**, sharing the experiences they had both had. Who should be trusted with this **INFORMATION**? Who would they use to **MOBILIZE** a **COURSE OF ACTION** to prevent the sky from falling? They needed a **LEADER** to guide them as they began to **PROMOTE** and **MARKET** the **SOLUTION** to animals of **INFLUENCE**, so that they could sell it to all animals that made up Animal-Kind. They realized that their leader had to be one who could provide leadership during a **CRISIS**.

That's when G-man realized Shuk-V would be perfect. This duck was always so concerned about bringing all   animals together for the greater good of everyone in the Kingdom.

When B-Girl and G-Man found him, Shuk-V was busy, as always, and was so very close to finishing his universal language product. He had spent late nights and early mornings dedicated to his purpose. He had gained respect for his willingness to hear from all animals, regardless of their shape, size, or color. His main interest was in creating a language that everyone could use to understand each other's thoughts, feelings, and needs.

Shuk-V listened to the story told by B-Girl and G-man. He quickly realized that the sky falling would pose a great challenge for everyone, and that he needed do something right away.

SHUK-V

Immediately, Shuk-V fell backwards upon his back and hind-feathers, placed his webbed feet firmly up in the air, and spread his small wings out as far as he could. When they saw this, although they did not understand, G-Man and B-Girl laid down next to him because they cared enough to share in what Shuk-V cared for. They believed in his abilities.

Very soon, all of the animals in the jungle had joined them, lying on their backs with their legs, paws, and wings spread as high as they could hold them. When the V-Crew saw this cooperation, it made them very happy. They finally asked Shuk-V to explain the reason why they were doing this.

With a very serious face and a strong voice, Shuk-V spoke with great determination.

"The sky may fall all around us, but it will not fall upon us, because WE ARE HOLDING UP OUR OWN END!"

This simple plan quickly spread across the world. Even the birds who could fly long distances flew upside down to help hold up the sky from falling.

The sky never fell upon any of them, and it never will, because whenever it seemed like someone's sky was getting ready to come crashing down, there was always someone else close by to help them **HOLD UP THEIR OWN END**.

Everyone found strength to hold up the sky because they followed the example of Shuk-V in taking the responsibility to say: "HOLD UP YOUR OWN END".

THE LIL VMAN'S PLEDGE AGAINST VIOLENCE

WILL YOU MAKE THIS PLEDGE AGAINST VIOLENCE?

I claim victory over violence in my life.

I claim victory over violence in my home and community.

I claim victory over violence in my school.

I pledge to team up with other people who claim non-violence,

KNOWING THAT EVEN ONE PERSON

CAN MAKE A DIFFERENCE!

HOW WELL DID YOU READ AND LISTEN?

Comprehension Activity (K – grade 6)

Try to answer these questions:

1. Who is the hero that lives in the World of Kids?

2. Do you remember the name of the group that helped Lil V?

3. What were the names of the V-Crew?

4. What was the problem that B-Girl discovered?

5. Who did the animals choose as a good leader for them to help solve their problem?

6. Why do you think the other animals chose him?

7. What was the solution the Shuck-V Duck came up with?

8. How did this affect the other animals in the jungle?

9. What was the result of everyone working together?

10. What is the lesson that we can learn from this story?

11. How can we make good choices in a group and help create good situations?

12. What can each one of us do as individuals to help make good choices and change negative situations into positive ones?

WHAT HAPPENED IN LIL VMAN'S STORY?

SEQUENCING

ORDINAL AND CARDINAL

NUMBERS

(K – 1st grade)

Directions: In each box, draw a picture of what happened in the story. In box 1, show what happened firstly. In box 2, show what happened secondly. In box 3, show what happened thirdly, and in box 4 show what was the last thing that happened in the story.

What is the first big thing that happened IN THE STORY?

1

What is the second big thing that happened IN THE STORY?

2

What is the third big thing that happened IN THE STORY?

3

HOW DID THE STORY END?

What is the last big thing that happened IN THE STORY?

4

WHAT DID YOU LEARN FROM THE STORY?

5

HOW WELL DID YOU READ?

Reading Comprehension Activity
(Intermediate)

1. Re-read the paragraph that begins with, "The plan was a big secret…". Name and explain at least three negative behaviors listed in this paragraph.

2. In your own words, explain what the PROBLEM is in the story.

3. Using the paragraph that begins with the words, "B-girl and G-man formed an immediate…", re-read and pronounce the words that are written in capital letters and bold print. Write these ten words on paper and use a dictionary to find and write the definition for each word.

4. **Find the resolution of the problem presented in this story and explain what the characters did to help resolve the problem.**

5. **Now practice your writing skills while RETELLING and SUMMARIZING the story. Remember that when you *retell* a story, you use the characters' actual dialogue, and specific details exactly as they were stated in the story. When you *summarize* a story, you simply paraphrase or describe events in the story in your own words.**

THE STORY (Grades 3-6)

Do you know the difference between **Retelling** and **Summarizing** a story? This will help you.

Retelling: Tell the story, repeating the details and words exactly as they are in the story. (Quote dialogue when you can.)
Summarizing: Briefly tell the story, giving the main points of the story using your own words and not words from the story.

RETELL "THE STORY OF LIL VMAN AND THE V-CREW":

_____

_____

_____

_____

_____

_____

SUMMARIZE "THE STORY OF LIL VMAN AND THE V-CREW":

_____

_____

_____

_____

_____

_____

_____

Use Who You Are!

We all must never forget one important thing if we want to live happy and peaceful lives: EVERYONE has something to offer this world.

The fact that each and every one of us is unique makes what we are more special and precious. The fact that we think, feel, respond, act, talk, walk, and look differently makes who we are more special and important. Just as the different pieces in a puzzle make the puzzle unique, our uniqueness makes us essential to completing the beauty of the world. Ultimately, we all must learn to respect, embrace, and appreciate the differences in ourselves and others.

Love who YOU are!
Respect who YOU are!
Embrace who YOU are!

No one can ever take your place. Even if someone looks and acts just like you, they will only be an imitation of you. You are the only one of you. There can never be another you! Explain this:

_____

_____

_____

LIL VMAN

NAME: LIL VMAN

CHALLENGES: HE IS BLIND. HE HAS

SPECIAL NEEDS.

UNIQUE QUALITIES: HE IS MULTICULTURAL AND "SEES" WITH HIS HEART.

What did Lil VMan use to help save the world and make the world a better place?

_____

_____

What does "multicultural" mean?

_____

_____

What does it mean to "see with your heart"? Why is this important?

_____

_____

_____

_____

B-GIRL

NAME: B-GIRL

CHALLENGES: SHE DOES NOT CONNECT WELL WITH OTHERS.

SHE ALWAYS FLIES HIGHER THAN ANYONE ELSE AND FLIES ALONE.

UNIQUE QUALITIES: SHE IS OBSERVANT (HAS A KEEN EYE)

AND IS AN EXCELLENT LISTENER.

What did B-Girl use to help save the world and make the world a better place?

_____

What does the statement "Does not connect well with others because she always flies higher" mean?

_____

_____

How can having a "keen eye" be helpful to you and others?

_____

_____

G-MAN

NAME: G-MAN

CHALLENGES: HIS SIZE IS DIFFERENT FROM OTHERS AROUND HIM.

UNIQUE QUALITIES: HE CAN RELATE WELL TO EVERYONE.

What did G-Man use to help save the world and make the world a better place?

_____

_____

What does it mean to be "different in size"? Does being a different size make a person bad?

_____

_____

What does it mean to "Relate well to everyone"? Why is it important to respect everyone?

_____

_____

_____

_____

SHUK-V

NAME: SHUK-V

CHALLENGES: HE DOES NOT FIT IN.

UNIQUE QUALITIES: HE IS CREATIVE. HE THINKS OUTSIDE OF THE BOX.

What did Shuk-V use to help save the world and make the world a better place?

_____

_____

What does "anti-social" mean? Do you have qualities and other people think are anti-social?

_____

_____

What does it mean to "think outside of the box"? Why is this important to be creative?

_____

_____

TIM-V

NAME: TIM-V TURTLE

CHALLENGES: HE MOVES AND THINKS SLOWER THAN OTHERS AROUND HIM. HE ENTERS AFTER EVERYONE.

UNIQUE QUALITIES: TIM ALWAYS FINISHES WHAT HE STARTS, NO MATTER HOW LONG IT TAKES. HE HAS AN EXCELLENT MEMORY.

Everyone moves, learns, and grows at a different rate. What does this mean?

_____

_____

_____

_____

_____

LIL VMAN AND THE V-CREW

(K – 2nd grade)
FIND THE WORDS YOU LEARNED ABOUT LIL VMAN AND THE V-CREW

```
G M A P Q P              N A J X H Z
M N N O K C              D U C K Z A
  Y I F E Y R            K E P T S D
  U M B F Z T            R G A D S R
    V J F W I Z          A O O A D K
    V W A N Z J          U W O J L Y
      F R W N A J        Q V T D N O
      O I I E P Y        V G E Z G H
        G F N P K Y      L G P N U G
        C A E I O J      H Q L K D C
          O R X S T M    E R O F L C
          E G H H W D    V E F A Y A
            Y A H A L M  I I D O G Q
            O G M I R P  L T A I L H
              Y T I O J Y  R T A E R C
              L Y V W E L  H G G L S Y
                F K D X T W  I J K E P A
                Y L U G M J  Q G R N C M
                  W B L I N D E W O E U V
                  Q Y D S P O S I T I V E
                    T Z Q C T E R C E S
                    D H P F O D S S E D
                      J B L P H V J I
                      C R E W C F R A
                        G L C G K T
                        E A G L E R
                          U A X H
                          V T Q G
```

• WORLD	• GOOD	• ENERGY
• SKY	• POSITIVE	• NEGATIVE
• EAGLE	• NETWORK	• SECRET
• DUCK	• GIRAFFE	• LEADER
• BLIND	• CREW	• HOLD

LIL VMAN AND THE V-CREW
(PUZZLE ANSWER KEY)
FIND THE WORDS YOU LEARNED ABOUT LIL VMAN AND THE V-CREW

```
G M A P Q P                                    N A J X H Z
M N N O K C                                    D U C K Z A
  Y I F E Y R                                  K E P T S D
U M B F Z T                                    R G A D S R
  V J F W I Z                                  A O O A D K
  V W A N Z J                                  U W O J L Y
  F R W N A J                                  Q V T D N O
  O I I E P Y                                  V G E Z G H
  G F N P K Y                                  L G P N U G
  C A E I O J                                  H Q L K D C
    O R X S T M                              E R O F L C
    E G H H W D                              V E F A Y A
    Y A H A L M                              I I D O G Q
    O G M I R P                              L T A I L H
      Y T I O J Y                            R T A E R C
      L Y V W E L                            H G G L S Y
      F K D X T W                            I J K E P A
      Y L U G M J                          Q G R N C M
        W B L I N D E W O E U V
        Q Y D S P O S I T I V E
          T Z Q C T E R C E S
          D H P F O D S S E D
          J B L P H V J I
          C R E W C F R A
          G L C G K T
          E A G L E R
            U A X H
            V T Q G
```

- WORLD
- SKY
- EAGLE
- DUCK
- BLIND

- GOOD
- POSITIVE
- NETWORK
- GIRAFFE
- CREW

- ENERGY
- NEGATIVE
- SECRET
- LEADER
- HOLD

LIL VMAN AND THE V-CREW
INTERMEDIATE
FIND THE WORDS YOU LEARNED ABOUT LIL VMAN AND V-CREW

```
        E N Z D L                        N T X H G
      O I R V A K N                    G E V U L J M
    U N P X D O E P F W              L E U M V X B P Z S
  D P T O J W G S N O J T          D W R K N S I C U R O U
  E E H S V A F Y O E K P E      W G B K S A U K T K Q Q E
Z T A C W T M M A I E R B H H O X L A Y W I O B V I E M D P
R A E W I N F L C T G W J C T P M E T U I S Q B O F S F F R
O C H V X O J D B U D B A Q P G V A Z G I L H S Y R P O E E
J I E P O R U Z D L T R T J A S N D C Z R L W C V K I M P V
O D X Z E Z L U F O D C X Z O B R E B J D Z J F R L J B A E
M E Z O K U V F E S I O A S T O X R R G F W U O J O U A J N
X D E U I C O S L N Q Z A P G R R S W T D Q H I D P N F A T
Y C C M D U D Z J P Z E W D Z N H H C G S H L P H X S N Q K
  S F N O Z L C L B A C T I O N A I Y C R D O B E R V W C
  V D M Z B D U F R N C O I V X B P U N P J O C B X C R W
    C C T Z I O H J M X X S E V I E C N E U L F N I E A
    A Q N U L S C H X A K E R L J A V N A U N Z A U
      Z B W G I E Y A S U D N I K N A M W V L T H
        O Q O C Z Z R A B K J T F H N M F Y I C
          W R G J E X R H I B Y D N I L B V I
          L H Z O T H I K Q F V H F Z E E
            B X U M Y C Q K Q F T A L A
            H E L Z J S X D T K M O
              Y G K B L F B Q X F
              Q H V W C L G U
                M Y C Y S J
                  B Y Y P
                  V W
```

- POSITIVE
- PREVENT
- INFLUENCE
- ABILITY

- NEGATIVE
- MOBILIZE
- BLIND
- DEDICATED

- MANKIND
- ACTION
- STRENGTH

- CREATIVE
- SOLUTION
- LEADERSHIP

LIL VMAN AND THE V-CREW
INTERMEDIATE (ANSWER KEY)
FIND THE WORDS YOU LEARNED ABOUT LIL VMAN AND THE V-CREW

```
        E N Z D L                               N T X H G
       O I R V A K N                          G E V U L J M
      U N P X D O E P F W                    L E U M V X B P Z S
     D P T O J W G S N O J T              D W R K N S I C U R O U
     E E H S V A F Y O E K P E           W G B K S A U K T K Q Q E
   Z T A C W T M M A I E R B H H O X L A Y W I O B V I E M D P
   R A E W I N F L C T G W J C T P M E T U I S Q B O F S F F R
   O C H V X O J D B U D B A Q P G V A Z G I L H S Y R P O E E
   J I E P O R U Z D L T R T J A S N D C Z R L W C V K I M P V
   O D X Z E Z L U F O D C X Z O B R E B J D Z J F R L J B A E
   M E Z O K U V F E S I O A S T O X R R G F W U O J O U A J N
   X D E U I C O S L N Q Z A P G R R S W T D Q H I D P N F A T
   Y C C M D U D Z J P Z E W D Z N H H C G S H L P H X S N Q K
   S F N O Z L C L B A C T I O N A I Y C R D O B E R V W C
   V D M Z B D U F R N C O I V X B P U N P J O C B X C R W
     C C T Z I O H J M X X S E V I E C N E U L F N I E A
     A Q N U L S C H X A K E R L J A V N A U N Z A U
       Z B W G I E Y A S U D N I K N A M W V L T H
        O Q O C Z Z R A B K J T F H N M F Y I C
         W R G J E X R H I B Y D N I L B V I
          L H Z O T H I K Q F V H F Z E E
            B X U M Y C Q K Q F T A L A
            H E L Z J S X D T K M O
             Y G K B L F B Q X F
             Q H V W C L G U
               M Y C Y S J
                B Y Y P
                 V W
```

- POSITIVE
- PREVENT
- INFLUENCE
- ABILITY

- NEGATIVE
- MOBILIZE
- BLIND
- DEDICATED

- MANKIND
- ACTION
- STRENGTH

- CREATIVE
- SOLUTION
- LEADERSHIP

WHEN

SELF-ESTEEM

GOES UP

GOES DOWN

I YAM WHAT I YAM!

For over seventy-five years, Popeye has been the hero that we think of when we want to see the bully finally get what he deserves. For a number of generations across the world, Popeye has been getting up from fights, scraping himself off of the ground, and coming out the winner over the worst bullies we could imagine.

For many children, it didn't matter that he had many challenges. As a matter of fact, it was probably because he had so many problems that he was so easy to identify with. Popeye dealt with all the following challenges:

- Extremely unattractive features
- Funnily-shaped body
- Big nose
- Partially blind (only had one good eye)
- Terrible speech problem
- Minimal intelligence
- Smoking and drinking
- Baldness (only had one strand of hair)
- Picked on constantly by all types of bullies
- Abandoned by his father as a child
- Only one friend, Wimpy, who was a cowardly "moocher"
- A girlfriend, Olive Oyl, who was easily impressed by every man that passed her way.

Popeye had to constantly prove himself to her over and over again.

Although Popeye had these challenges, he was always very proud of who he was. Popeye always <u>stayed true to who he was and what he believed</u>. At the end of the day, he had won every fight, won his girlfriend, and had everyone on his side. HE WON! In spite of the fact that he was NOT attractive, popular, strong, smart, or perfect, HE STILL WON.

Now, what about you? When you take a good look at yourself, what can you honestly say about yourself? Do you understand that it is alright not to be perfect or popular?

BE PROUD OF WHO YOU ARE! Everyone should be able to look in the mirror and say **"I YAM WHAT I YAM!"** **and know that it is a GOOD thing!**

Why do think it is important to be proud of who you are?

_____

_____

_____

How and why does believing that you are important help your self-esteem?

_____

_____

_____

If Popeye didn't like himself, what would you say to him to change his mind?

_____

_____

_____

Do you have good self-esteem? What can you say to yourself to improve your self-esteem?

_____

_____

_____

BE PROUD OF WHO YOU ARE!

I YAM WHAT I YAM!

(2 -6 grades)

What are some of the special traits that make you who you are?

_____

_____

_____

Are there other members in your family who have these special features? Who are they?

_____

_____

Popeye had some personal traits that were a challenge for him. Do you have any personal traits that are a challenge to you sometimes? Describe them. Explain why they are a challenge to you.

_____

_____

_____

_____

Now, share your answers with another classmate. Ask your classmate to explain what they think of your special traits and your challenges. Write their answer on the lines below.

_____

_____

_____

_____

How do you feel about the responses you received from your classmates?

_____

_____

_____

_____

Now, take this worksheet home and share it with your family. Ask for their responses to this worksheet, and write their responses below.

_____

_____

_____

_____

_____

I YAM WHAT I YAM! (K – 1st grade)

Draw a portrait of yourself. Don't forget to include all of the special traits that make you who you are.

61

THE TALE OF HONEY BIZZIE BEE

A LESSON ABOUT BULLYING AND SELF-ESTEEM

There once was a bumble bee whose name was Betty. Her friends just used the first letter of her name combined with her talents and simply called her "Honey B." They really could have called her "Honey Betty" or "Betty Honey", or "Betty, the girl who makes the honey", but they made it simple and just called her "Honey B."

Honey B did not have much of a social life. She did not attend many of the parties and events held in the insect and animal kingdom, yet everyone knew of her work of making honey from the pollen of flowers.

Each year, all of the bears from all over the forests would come seeking out her tree just to get a taste of that year's honey. They, of course, would get their noses stung, but when asked if it was worth it, they would always say, "Yes!"

Honey B was a queen bumble bee who was too young to go into retirement. She had produced thousands of children bees who carried out the task of reconstructing their home each year after the cold of winter.

Although Honey B was busy, busy, busy all year long, her busiest season was in the spring. You could always find her going from flower to flower, making her buzzing sound. She would taste each flower and then send message to all of her troops by doing her wonderful **"Bee dance."** Honey B made the most fabulous figure eight's in the entire colony! Oh what a worker Honey B was! Without her message, the bees would not take action, and the flowers would not be pollinated.

Now Honey Bee's work pollinating flowers was not only crucial to her bee colony, it was also crucial to rest of the insects and even the people who lived in the land where Honey B lived. Without her helping to pollinate the flowers, there would be no seeds for new flowers or trees which produce the tasty fruit and vegetables eaten by insects, animals, and mankind. As a matter of fact, all of the insects and animals in the world needed the plants to live and grow in order for them to have the oxygen which they all needed to live. If the animals did not have the plants, they could not breathe or produce baby animals and insects. Honey B knew that the **scientists had discovered that after seven days without bee-pollination, everything would begin to die**. What a great responsibility Honey B had! She had to get that message out each and every day through Buzz-ology and Figure-eight-ology, which

is the Internet of the bee world.

It probably seems as if everything in Honey B's world was just fine, but disaster would have struck had it not been for the H.U.Y.O.E. Team. One would think that when you do as much good for everyone as Honey B did, that everyone would be happy and supportive, but that is not the case. Here is that story.

There were some who were very jealous of anything or anyone who seemed to get more attention than they did. In order to feel bigger and more important, they became bullies. They said negative things about other insects or animals and made fun of them. Although many of these insects and animals felt very hurt by the cruel things that were said, they had to learn to stick together. They won many of their battles against the evil and negative spirits of those who tried to hurt them by following the **H.U.Y.O.E. principle that simply encouraged them not to give up, but to always "Hold Up Your Own End"** and **"Do unto others as you want others to do to you."** They realized that they could have the feeling of victory simply by not returning evil for evil.

Honey B was always being picked on by Harry Hornet and Wally Wasp. These two bullies were well known in the insect world. They were sleek, trim, and strong. They always looked like they had just finished working out in the gym. Their bodies were slim, and they had large wings that could fly very fast and even hover like a helicopter before taking off full speed towards a target. They looked completely different than Honey B who had a very large body and small wings.

Even though Honey B's wings were small and some people had even said that it was **scientifically and aerodynamically impossible for her to fly,** she had just been too busy helping the insect and animal kingdoms to consider that she had birth defects to overcome. She had simply grown up from a baby bee and learned how to fly by watching her parents do it.

Honey B had never thought about how small her wings were in comparison to her body until Walter Wasp and Harry Hornet began to make her life miserable every day. It seemed that every where she went, they followed her, making fun of her. They told her that there was no way that she should be able to fly because the scientist said her wings were too small for her body.

However, Harry Hornet and Wally Wasp did not know that **everything that is born and lives is already perfect for its own destiny and service to its part of the planet**. You see, no matter how we look, or how we are made, we all have a special purpose and place in this world.

The H.U.Y.O.E. team knew this and spread this message wherever they went. They were able to encourage Honey B just in the nick of time. Honey B had begun to listen to the bad things being said about her. She had begun to have doubts about her own abilities and even questioned if being born was a mistake. She wondered if she was supposed to fly. Honey B, unfortunately, did not eat or work. She stopped doing what she did best.

When Honey B stopped working, the other bees stopped doing what they needed to do also. As predicted, the animal kingdom began to suffer. The H.U.Y.O.E. Team needed to help before things got worse, so they planned a surprise party to honor Honey B for all of her accomplishments. Everyone there lifted Honey B's spirits and let her know that they needed her contributions to their society. Wally Wasp and Harry Hornet finally realized that everyone and everything created is important to the fragile balance of nature, and that the destruction of any part affects all.

Now you can see Honey B going from flower to flower, happily doing her job. Every now and then, she stops to smell a human before flying on back to work. And if you hear her buzzing, you don't have to be afraid. **Honey B's only concern is to spread the crucial message: do what you are created to do and never forget to "Hold Up Your Own End!"**

THE END

ACTIVITIES AND DISCUSSION QUESTIONS FOR

THE TALE OF HONEY BIZZIE BEE

(ALL GRADES)

1. Listen to the entire story of Honey Bizzie Bee. First <u>retell</u> the story, then <u>summarize</u> it.

2. Show that you understand the personality of Honey Bizzie Bee as being helpful by naming something that people do when they are being helpful to others.

3. Name at least two positive characteristics about Honey Bizzie Bee, and tell why this makes her a helpful character.

4. Discuss the disproportioned shape of a honey bee. Point out that Honey Bee's disproportionate in size and shape in the picture.

   Older students should learn the actual insect body parts of the honey bee and be able to name them. Research can also be done regarding the effects of the disproportionate size of the honey bee.

5. Discuss the attitudes of Walter Wasp and Harry Hornet.

6. Name at least two negative behaviors that are exhibited by Walter and Harry in the story.

7. State what the problem is in this story.

8. Discuss how you think Honey Bizzie Bee feels about what is being said about her.

   a. Discuss what it means to have good self-esteem.

   b. Discuss why it is important to feel good about who you are.

   c. Discuss why it is important to respect the differences we all have.

   d. Discuss the importance of respecting other people's challenges.

9. Discuss the resolution of the problem presented in this story and why this resolution is appropriate.

10. Discuss the feelings regarding self-esteem that are generated from this story and feelings that we feel because of the people in our lives.

11. Discuss appropriate solutions that can be implemented when our self-esteem is affected in a negative way. Positive solutions should be emphasized.

12. How does the concept of holding up your own end relate to self-esteem?

Write a short follow-up story about Honey Bizzie Bee showing what happened after she learned to appreciate herself. Be sure to show how her self-concept affected others.

_____

_____

_____

_____

_____

_____

_____

AMAZING H.U.Y.O.E. MAZES

PLEASE HELP HONEY BIZZIE BEE FIND HAPPINESS!

SELF-ESTEEM – FRAGILE: HANDLE WITH CARE

(INTERMEDIATE)

SELF-ESTEEM IS THE CONFIDENCE AND SATISFACTION A PERSON HAS IN ONESELF.

Your self-esteem can change very easily, depending on what is happening to you and who you are with. What is your level of self-esteem like right now? Explain why you feel this way.

_____

_____

_____

_____

Who do you associate with that makes you feel important, confident, unique, and accepted? Why is this person good for your self-esteem? Is this a mutual feeling? How do you know?

_____

_____

_____

_____

_____

Has there been a time when you did not feel confident, happy, or satisfied with yourself? What made you feel this way? Describe exactly how you felt.

_____

_____

_____

Can you remember a time when you made someone else feel this way? Explain what happened.

_____

_____

_____

Did you apologize to the person whose self-esteem you may have harmed? What did you say?

_____

_____

_____

SELF-ESTEEM – FRAGILE:

HANDLE WITH CARE

(INTERMEDIATE)

A SINCERE APOLOGY IS A SURE SIGN OF MATURITY AND HUMANITY.

Never be afraid to apologize for hurting someone else. It shows strength and earnest concern for the well-being of other people. If your apology is sincere, the rewards will be felt by everyone. The purpose of a sincere apology is to promote the healing of the person you hurt or harmed.

Which of the following statements are the beginnings of a sincere apology?

I am truly sorry for… _____   I am truly sorry that you feel that way… _____

I am sorry that you misunderstood… _____   I spoke out of turn… _____

If you feel bad about what I said… _____   Will you please forgive me for… _____

Why are some of these apologies, and why are some of them not?

_____

_____

_____

_____

Think of someone that you have hurt or harmed. Write a sincere apology to that person. Remember, it is a sincere apology when you clearly express why <u>you</u> were wrong and if you express <u>your</u> sincere remorse and regret for what you did. A sincere apology can help increase and heal the self-esteem of others, as well as your own. Now, write your sincere apology on the lines provided. Do not forget to address the problem in detail. Explain why you feel you handled the situation incorrectly, and explain why you feel the way you do right now.

_____

_____

_____

_____

_____

_____

_____

_____

CONGRATULATIONS! IT TAKES A PERSON WHO IS STONG IN

CHARACTER TO MAKE A <u>SINCERE</u> APOLOGY TO OTHERS.

SELF- ESTEEM - INTERMEDIATE

Find the words about self-esteem.

```
        L P P J U                              O W P C C
      Y J D X D W R                          Z D I H C H Q
    O A R S X K Z A T G                    Y R Q X O N E B F J
   N R A Y R Z G T F C Q B                A V O N G I Y Z G Z S J
  G N I D N A T S R E D N U              D K I N D N E S S H I E W
 X W V W H W E R F S P M X C F A G K B R R I S J I Y Y C L O
 X Y Z H B N Q N O E S O E P H P P J D L I D W T A X X N L F
 H W K B T M B C L Z E S E T G P X O O H Y F V E T M T E Y F
 R G S I C S I C T T R S G C A J C A L S V E O V U T Z D A B
 T I O A B E J M J C U E T I F E T Y Q O J E R O D W Q I O D
 G N L L T P U D T B K N O A P Z G A A P G V B L F M C F J Y
 W U J Y E I B R H D N I I P X J D X Q L Z Y J T Z F D N C R
 W X F Y H C S V G I D P N Q Z D J H R N N O S H M J M O X G
  P R I H E N F I H P P C P U K J M O M E E T S E G G C B
  H V P S V L E I B N A E A W E A B B Z F H S B M G Y R H
   V W P P H P R E W H A C C O M P L I S H M E N T S Q
    D F T Y E F E D I X Y N X C R B O O U C A D W C
     U L D B A U F O F H K Z W F Y N C G D E C W
      H B P L Y L F I P I M P O R T A N T Q B
       I Y E N V A I B K G F C G O B P S J
        S E A N A L D V V E E M K E A Y
         R L F D X O Q X J A A C V C
          S E G N E L L A H C T F
           M G V R H K J A A H
             E S I H S D Y C
              B K X R U L
               Y G K D
                V B
```

- CONFIDENCE
- HELPFUL
- ACCEPTED
- KINDNESS
- HAPPINESS
- DIFFERENCE
- ESTEEM
- IMPORTANT
- SATISFIED
- UNDERSTANDING
- CHALLENGES
- ACCOMPLISHMENTS
- APOLOGY
- UNIQUE
- ATTENTION
- LOVE
- RESPECT
- SOCIETY

SELF-ESTEEM - INTERMEDIATE

ANSWER KEY

```
        L P P J U                          O W P C C
      Y J D X D W R                      Z D I H C H Q
    O A R S X K Z A T G                Y R Q X O N E B F J
  N R A Y R Z G T F C Q B              A V O N G I Y Z G Z S J
  G N I D N A T S R E D N U        D K I N D N E S S H I E W
X W V W H W E R F S P M X C F A G K B R R I S J I Y Y C L O
X Y Z H B N Q N O E S O E P H P P J D L I D W T A X X N L F
H W K B T M B C L Z E S E T G P X O O H Y F V E T M T E Y F
R G S I C S I C T T R S G C A J C A L S V E O V U T Z D A B
T I O A B E J M J C U E T I F E T Y Q O J E R O D W Q I O D
G N L L T P U D T B K N O A P Z G A A P G V B L F M C F J Y
W U J Y E I B R H D N I I P X J D X Q L Z Y J T Z F D N C R
W X F Y H C S V G I D P N Q Z D J H R N N O S H M J M O X G
  P R I H E N F I H P P C P U K J M O M E E T S E G G C B
  H V P S V L E I B N A E A W E A B B Z F H S B M G Y R H
    V W P P H P R E W H A C C O M P L I S H M E N T S Q
      D F T Y E F E D I X Y N X C R B O O U C A D W C
      U L D B A U F O F H K Z W F Y N C G D E C W
      H B P L Y L F I P I M P O R T A N T Q B
      I Y E N V A I B K G F C G O B P S J
      S E A N A L D V V E E M K E A Y
      R L F D X O Q X J A A C V C
      S E G N E L L A H C T F
      M G V R H K J A A H
      E S I H S D Y C
      B K X R U L
      Y G K D
      V B
```

Name _____

SELF-ESTEEM

Please unscramble the words below

1. voel _____

2. spsapnieh _____

3. ceganhell _____

4. cear _____

5. tedirefnf _____

6. psterce _____

7. aslecip _____

8. tmseee _____

9. slef _____

10. lpfhleu _____

11. ueqinu _____

12. nintfdeco _____

13. tcaecp _____

14. efrovgi _____

15. gpoaoyl _____

16. sonhte _____

17. reicesn _____

18. lhae _____

ANSWER KEY: SELF-ESTEEM

1. love _____

2. happiness _____

3. challenge _____

4. care _____

5. different _____

6. respect _____

7. special _____

8. esteem _____

9. self _____

10. helpful _____

11. unique _____

12. confident _____

13. accept _____

14. forgive _____

15. apology _____

16. honest _____

17. sincere _____

18. heal _____

SUPER PEOPLE!

Lil V

Popeye

YOU!

(Draw your picture here.)

WHAT IS VIOLENCE?

VIOLENCE IS ANY ACT OF INTENTIONAL HARM OR DESTRUCTION UPON ONESELF OR OTHERS.

HANDS THAT HURT SOMEONE = VIOLENCE (K – 1st grade)

HITTING

PUSHING

BULLYING

GRABBING

BAD TOUCHING

HANDS THAT HURT SOMEONE
= VIOLENCE (K – 1st grade)

This how I feel when I am hit.

This is how I feel when I am pushed.

HANDS THAT HURT SOMEONE
= VIOLENCE (K – 1st grade)

This how I feel when I am bullied.

This is how I feel when I am grabbed.

HANDS THAT HURT SOMEONE
= VIOLENCE (K – 1st grade)

This how I feel when someone touches me the wrong way.

THIS IS HOW I ASK FOR HELP.

BULLYING!

Bullying is a VERY serious problem that affects children of all ages every day.

Four out of every five children say that they have been bullied.

- Bullying can make children feel hurt, scared, sick, lonely, embarrassed, and very sad. Bullying has even caused the death of some children.

- Bullies hit, kick, or push to hurt people, or they use words to call names, threaten, tease, or scare other people.

- A bully says mean things about someone, grabs other children's stuff, makes fun of someone, or leaves a child out of the group on purpose.

- Bullies threaten people or try to make others do things they don't want to do.

- A bully makes another person feel like they are not a good person or that they are not worth having around.

- Bullying can last a long time unless people do something to help.

BULLYING CAN BE STOPPED !

ARE YOU BEING BULLIED?

It hurts to be picked on. It hurts when people isolate you and make you feel bad about yourself. Here is a list of things that people sometimes experience when they are being bullied. Put a check next to any situations that may be occurring in your life.

_____ I am scared, and I am afraid of being hurt by someone.

_____ I feel angry, and I want to hurt the person who is bullying me.

_____ I wonder if anyone will ever help me.

_____ I feel like running away from home.

_____ Perhaps I deserve to be bullied because of who I am.

_____ Perhaps I am being bullied because of something I did to someone else.

_____ I really feel helpless. But, if I let anyone know that I am afraid, I will still be bullied.

_____ I wonder if this will go on forever.

_____ Sometimes I pretend that I am someone else or somewhere else until the bullying stops.

_____ I do not deserve to be treated like this. No one deserves this type of treatment.

_____ Sometimes I wonder if anyone notices or understands what is happening to me.

_____ I wish that I could trade places with the bully so that I could hurt that person.

_____ If I had someone to talk with and really trust, things would be different.

BULLYING WARNING SIGNS!

	PHYSICAL BULLY	EMOTIONAL BULLY	VERBAL BULLY	SEXUAL BULLY
K - 2	Hitting, pushing, biting, kicking, fighting, slapping	Exclusion, ignoring, isolation, rejection, teasing, humiliation, fear	Name-calling, disrespectfulness, interrupting, refusing to listen, loud talking,	Bathroom aggression and intrusions regarding privacy issues
3 - 6	Hitting, pushing, biting, kicking, fighting, slapping	Exclusion, ignoring, isolation, rejection, teasing, defamation of character, humiliation, fear	Name-calling, insults, disrespectfulness, interrupting, refusing to listen, loud talking, profanity, lies	Mobbing, inappropriate touching and displays
7 - 1 2	Gang initiations and wars, mobbing, fighting, physical aggression and mortal harm, retaliation, fear tactics	Profanity, coercion, isolation, ostracizing, manipulation, abandonment, defamation of character, fear	Name-calling, insults, disrespectfulness, interrupting, refusing to listen, loud talking, profanity, defamation of character, lies	Gang initiations, date rape, peer promiscuity, provocative apparel, inappropriate touching

It is very important to be able to recognize the signs of bullying and abuse in all circumstances.

Discuss the chart and find the terms that apply to you. What have you learned from this chart?

_____

_____

_____

_____

_____

IS IT VIOLENCE?

(grades 3 - 6)

Read each situation and determine if it is violence. Explain why you think it is or is not violence.

1. A big kid keeps a smaller kid from getting into the lunchroom by physically blocking the entrance.

_____

_____

_____

_____

2. You walk down the hallway and shove someone out of your way.

_____

_____

_____

_____

3. Someone spits on another person.

_____

_____

_____

_____

4. You text a message to someone in which you threaten to beat them up.

_____

_____

_____

5. A couple of kids corner another kid in the lavatory and demand that he or she give them money.

_____

_____

_____

IS IT VIOLENCE?

(Intermediate)

Read each situation and determine if it is violence. Explain why you think it is or is not violence.

1. A boyfriend and girlfriend are having a disagreement. When she tries to walk away, he grabs her arm and won't let her go.

_____

_____

_____

_____

2. Someone forces another person to kiss them but does not have sex with them.

_____

_____

_____

_____

3. While yelling nasty insults and calling names, two or three people follow behind someone that is walking.

_____

_____

_____

_____

4. A person continually calls another person's phone late at night to wake them and then hangs up.

_____

_____

_____

_____

5. A girl hits a boy whenever she gets mad, but he does not hit her back.

_____

_____

_____

_____

ARE YOU A BULLY?

Do you do some of these things?	Tease, hurt other people's feelings; Hit, push, threaten or intimidate others; Make fun of others; insult other people; Damage other peoples things or steal from others; Call people names; tell lies about other people.
Do you think you are:	Stronger than anyone else? Smarter than anyone else? Street Smart?
Think about this: Friends are people that support each other when they have problems. Friends have fun. People feel good about themselves when they help each other. Friends don't blame others for their problems.	Would you like to have some support? Would you like someone to say "Hey, do you want some help?" Do you have fun and feel good later when you think about what you have done? Would you like to feel good about yourself? If you do something wrong, what would take more guts: blaming someone else or being strong and discussing the situation?
If you would like to change, and have friends, here are a few tips:	ASK FOR HELP. Take responsibility for your own actions. Laugh with people not at them. If you have problems that you can't work out for yourself or control, talk to and trust someone.

LIL VMAN SAYS:
LET'S STOP THE BULLYING!

PLEASE,

DISCUSS YOUR FEELINGS AND IDEAS ABOUT BULLYING.

BULLYING!

Write the letter of the correct match next to each statement.

1. _____ Bullying is wrong...

   a. is the bully's biggest weapon.

2. _____ Do not try to deal with a bully on your own...

   b. there is nothing wrong with asking for help.

3. _____ If you do nothing when you see someone being bullied...

   c. the bullying has nothing to do with you personally.

4. _____ Part of the satisfaction that bullies get...

   d. no matter what the age of the person.

5. _____ The single most important thing a school can do is...

   e. the bullies may think you approve of what they are doing.

   f. comes from the reaction of bystanders.

6. _____ Keeping things secret...

7. _____ When reporting a bully, don't exaggerate...

   g. you may be accused of being the bully.

8. _____ The best way to stop bullying at home or school is...

   h. it may throw doubt on everything you say.

9. _____ Do not hit a bully...

   i. talk openly to someone you trust.

   j. have a clear policy to which everyone is committed.

10. _____ Most of the time...

ANSWER KEY FOR "BULLYING" WORKSHEET

Write the letter of the correct match next to each statement.

1.	d	Bullying is wrong...	a.	is the bully's biggest weapon.
2.	b	Do not try to deal with a bully on your own...	b.	because there is nothing wrong with asking for help.
3.	e	If you do nothing when you see someone being bullied...	c.	the bullying has nothing to do with you personally.
4.	f	Part of the satisfaction that bullies get...	d.	no matter what the age of the person.
5.	j	The single most important thing a school can do is...	e.	the bullies may think you approve of what they are doing.
6.	a	Keeping things secret...	f.	comes from the reaction of bystanders.
7.	h	When reporting a bully, don't exaggerate...	g.	you may be accused of being the bully.
8.	i	The best way to stop bullying at home or school is...	h.	it may throw doubt on everything you say.
9.	g	Do not hit a bully...	i.	talk openly to someone you trust.
10.	c	Most of the time...	j.	have a clear policy to which everyone is committed.

WARNING SIGNS OF VIOLENCE (grades 3-6)

Find the words about the "Warning Signs of Violence"

```
D  Q  Y  R  G  H  C  E  M  F  L  Z  L  P  E  F  P  Y  R  Q
O  S  I  T  X  O  X  L  N  F  Z  V  V  N  G  I  X  T  E  P
J  F  C  U  M  E  R  Q  J  Q  E  D  J  C  N  D  R  G  A  D
O  D  B  E  T  E  W  W  U  H  O  B  H  W  I  G  H  E  S  U
N  R  G  G  H  S  K  U  P  T  V  G  W  R  H  E  N  S  S  J
Y  R  J  U  D  G  M  E  N  T  A  L  V  R  G  T  L  P  U  A
X  T  E  N  D  Q  E  T  D  L  J  F  I  L  I  I  E  N  R  W
T  A  A  K  C  A  B  D  E  E  F  G  A  W  S  N  G  U  I  P
Q  H  A  O  E  R  B  R  E  A  T  H  I  N  G  G  T  K  N  J
S  P  S  C  D  Q  D  O  T  H  R  E  A  T  E  N  I  N  G  C
O  F  T  P  F  C  E  J  A  O  I  A  C  U  E  R  A  J  O  E
K  M  S  V  C  D  Y  G  D  J  U  R  Z  R  W  M  A  M  Y  Z
G  I  O  T  E  W  Z  Y  G  E  B  H  V  A  F  G  F  U  O  C
N  B  N  U  S  R  J  N  D  F  J  O  Z  C  N  O  Y  J  R  D
I  C  F  C  P  F  I  T  E  I  U  Q  C  H  R  X  D  Y  J  J
B  V  Y  Q  A  N  O  X  H  S  U  K  L  T  J  X  I  Q  B  E
B  L  N  S  W  U  X  Z  N  A  P  O  I  F  Z  L  P  E  H  T
U  I  T  O  Q  P  Y  E  Y  M  U  N  C  D  C  I  A  G  T  C
R  E  R  J  Q  C  S  J  O  D  G  Y  E  C  F  C  R  O  P  Y
R  F  L  B  P  S  O  V  R  Y  X  K  O  C  W  Z  E  O  Z  E
```

ANXIETY	SIGHING	FIDGETING
NERVOUSNESS	FROWNING	RAPID
BREATHING	RUBBING	HANDS
SPIT	LOUD	FASTER
JUDGMENTAL	FEEDBACK	QUIET
THREATENING	REASSURING	COMFORTING

Name _____ Date: _____

WARNING SIGNS OF VIOLENCE

Please unscramble the words below related to the warning signs of violence.

1. SRTESS

_____

2. EDTVIUPSIR

_____

3. ORVAEHSIB

_____

4. SYIENIODGB

_____

5. AKTNLIG

_____

6. LDUO

_____

7. ITNRIUGERTNP

_____

8. SOICONVSERTNA

_____

9. GEIAVTNE

_____

10. NATINTOTE

_____

11. EACSASSTNI

_____

12. YDOB

_____

13. AGENGLUA

_____

14. RSNEACESRUA

_____

15. TFROOCM

_____

16. TERRIDCE

_____

17. CSOFU

_____

18. TYIIPVTOIS

_____

19. USFERE

_____

20. TCROAOEPE

_____

ANSWER KEY TO WORD SCRAMBLE

WARNING SIGNS OF VIOLENCE

1. STRESS
_____

2. DISRUPTIVE
_____

3. BEHAVIORS
_____

4. DISOBEYING
_____

5. TALKING
_____

6. LOUD
_____

7. INTERRUPTING
_____

8. CONVERSATIONS
_____

9. NEGATIVE
_____

10. ATTENTION
_____

11. ASSISTANCE
_____

12. BODY
_____

13. LANGUAGE
_____

14. REASSURANCE
_____

15. COMFORT
_____

16. REDIRECT
_____

17. FOCUS
_____

18. POSITIVITY
_____

19. REFUSE
_____

20. COOPERATE
_____

STOP! THINK! AND GROW!

When you are angry or upset, it is very easy to move, act, or react before you really think. We must learn how to slow down so that we can be in control of our own emotions and circumstances. We are going to learn some ways to stop what we are doing, think about the entire situation, and act maturely when we are feeling angry.

STOP! THINK! AND GROW!

When someone does something to harm you or make you angry, do three things **BEFORE** you do anything else. The first thing you must do is

STOP! Before you do or say hurtful things.

Sometimes stopping ourselves is not easy. It takes a strong person to STOP! before doing something that **seems like** it will make you feel better but you **know** that it is actually the wrong thing to do.

Has a parent, relative, teacher, or some other adult ever told you to STOP! How did it make you feel?

_____

_____

Draw a picture of what was happening when you were told to STOP!

Why was stopping the right thing to do?

_____

_____

_____

_____

STOP! THINK! AND GROW!

When someone does something to harm you or make you angry, do three things **BEFORE** you do anything else. The second thing you must do is

---

THINK! Before you do or say hurtful things.

When someone hurts us, we focus on what we **BELIEVE** the other person meant to do. Sometimes, we **misunderstand** what someone says or does to us.

If you do or say something to hurt someone else, it is usually because you think that the person deserves it. But, what if they do not really deserve to be hurt?

THINK! Is this an accident? Tell about when someone accidentally hurt you.

_____

_____

THINK! Have you ever thought someone lied to you, but they didn't? When?

_____

_____

THINK! Have you ever thought someone talked about you, but they didn't? When?

_____

_____

THINK! If I hurt someone, will it help? Why doesn't it help to get revenge?

_____

_____

_____

STOP! THINK! AND GROW!

When someone does something to harm you or make you angry, do three things **BEFORE** you do anything else. The third thing you must do is

> ## GROW! Before you do or say hurtful things.

When we were babies, we reacted to everything and everybody around us by doing whatever would bring us attention. As we grow up, we learn that being the center of attention is not always best. Having the last word or getting your way, does not necessarily mean that you win.

GROW! Why do people feel that they have to have the last word? Why do people feel that they must have their own way all of the time?

_____

_____

_____

GROW! If you are having a problem with someone, what can you do to show that you are growing up and not acting like a baby?

_____

_____

GROW! Tell about a time when you showed that you were growing up. How did you feel? How did the people around you feel? What will you do to grow more?

_____

_____

_____

STOP, THINK, AND GROW!

Find the hidden words.

```
            H Q
            S L
          F Z R T
          R J O V
        J U G E N M
        R M F H S R
      C T Y Y W N C B
      H V C T G V C Z
    U C I C K I O Z D G
    T H I N K O G Z D R
  A Q I N Z W D O I W W P
  I R U G Y B T B F L M S
I Q L A D O B N E S P Z V B
G S B P P G O E F J C H V E
E N I F F S H L D O T U L C L U
R Z R S M N A W I R T X Q S I Y
B U N M C C E T G C E H U W I E L U
W M W A H Q J T Z C R V T M Z V Q Z
O C O Z T J B P E Z A P A F E L E M Q H
Z M F E U D X F N Z X Q S Z L B B R Q F
Q I P R W R B U L T X W U K W B L O J L V W
U A C E L E F C K I X H T O O O R Q F V V H
I U O P G T U S J H O B T B Y B R E L K G B G A
S C U N N K X T E R N Q U Z X Y P N H A E V J D
P C L W A A E L B I A P O G S O N R N D B M V G W B
O M Y J R V Y R G S T U Y S K T A J I V V T O X U R
W T S U R T O K L Y T T X S J M O I S W V P G E Q D Y O
W S M N I O J P T U R F C A P J Y G G R O W S K Y C F I
M V P T J R Y P F A J V R E Q N B G K F T J S Z S G N H K M
K Z H D M O R C G I X W K V B N B J X R F V X K F V A P S N
```

- STOP
- ANGER
- ACCIDENT
- PROBLEM
- THINK
- BELIEVE
- ATTENTION
- MATURE
- GROW
- TRUST
- BEFORE
- WINNER

STOP, THINK, AND GROW! – ANSWER KEY

Find the hidden words.

```
                        H Q
                        S L
                      F Z R T
                      R J O V
                    J U G E N M
                    R M F H S R
                  C T Y Y W N C B
                  H V C T G V C Z
                U C I C K I O Z D G
                T H I N K O G Z D R
              A Q I N Z W D O I W W P
              I R U G Y B T B F L M S
            I Q L A D O B N E S P Z V B
            G S B P P G O E F J C H V E
          E N I F F S H L D O T U L C L U
          R Z R S M N A W I R T X Q S I Y
        B U N M C C E T G C E H U W I E L U
        W M W A H Q J T Z C R V T M Z V Q Z
      O C O Z T J B P E Z A P A F E L E M Q H
      Z M F E U D X F N Z X Q S Z L B B R Q F
    Q I P R W R B U L T X W U K W B L O J L V W
    U A C E L E F C K I X H T O O O R Q F V V H
  I U O P G T U S J H O B T B Y B R E L K G B G A
  S C U N N K X T E R N Q U Z X Y P N H A E V J D
P C L W A A E L B I A P O G S O N R N D B M V G W B
O M Y J R V Y R G S T U Y S K T A J I V V T O X U R
W T S U R T O K L Y T T X S J M O I S W P G E Q D Y O
W S M N I O J P T U R F C A P J Y G G R O W S K Y C F I
M V P T J R Y P F A J V R E Q N B G K F T J S Z S G N H K M
K Z H D M O R C G I X W K V B N B J X R F V X K F V A P S N
```

- STOP
- ANGER
- ACCIDENT
- PROBLEM
- THINK
- BELIEVE
- ATTENTION
- MATURE
- GROW
- TRUST
- BEFORE
- WINNER

TIM-V TURTLE SAYS: STOP, THINK, AND GROW!

WORDS THAT HURT SOMEONE =
VIOLENCE (K-1st grade)

LYING   TEASING   BULLYING

CUSSING   NAME-CALLING

WORDS THAT HURT SOMEONE =
VIOLENCE (K – 1st grade)

This how I feel when I am teased.

This is how I feel when someone puts me down.

WORDS THAT HURT SOMEONE = VIOLENCE (K – 1st grade)

This how I feel when someone talks mean to me.

This is how I feel when someone bosses me around.

WORDS THAT HURT SOMEONE = VIOLENCE (K – 1st grade)

This how I feel when someone curses at me.

This is how I feel when someone laughs at me to hurt me.

WORDS THAT HURT SOMEONE =
VIOLENCE (K – 1st grade)

This how I feel when someone says things about me that are not true.

THIS IS HOW I ASK FOR HELP.

THIS IS HOW I STOP WORDS
THAT = VIOLENCE (K – 1st grade)

This is how I stop teasing others people.

This is how I stop putting other people down.

THIS IS HOW I STOP WORDS
THAT = VIOLENCE (K – 1st grade)

This is how I stop talking mean to other people.

This is how I stop bossing other people around.

THIS IS HOW I STOP WORDS THAT = VIOLENCE (K – 1st grade)

This how I stop cursing at other people.

This is how i help others using my words.

THIS IS HOW I STOP WORDS
THAT = VIOLENCE (K – 1st grade)

This how I stop saying things that are not true about other people.

This is how I stop laughing at other people to hurt them.

SLOW YOUR ROLL!

(INTERMEDIATE ANGER MANAGEMENT)

When you are angry or upset, it is very easy to move, act, or react before you really

think. We must learn how to slow ourselves down so that we can be in control of our

own emotions and circumstances. We are going to learn some ways to slow ourselves

down when we are feeling angry or upset.

ANGER VS. FURY

We all get angry sometimes. Anger is a strong feeling of displeasure. You can be angry and still be in complete control of your thoughts and emotions. At the point of anger, you can make decisions about whether your next steps will lead to the following:

- Allow the situation to affect you in a greater manner

- Choose to diffuse the situation by not continuing to respond to it or let it affect you

Of course, the best choice is always to diffuse a potentially unpleasant situation by resolving it before it becomes a greater issue. By doing this, you can avoid the escalation of emotions that can lead to fury.

What is fury? Have you heard anyone say or have you said, "I was furious"? Let's look at that.

According to Webster's Ninth New Collegiate Dictionary, the definition of fury is "An intense, disordered, destructive rage." You might look at fury as being the difference between these two illustrations:

VS.

VS.

THIS IS ANGER   THIS IS FURY!

1. Describe the difference between anger and fury.

   _____

   _____

   _____

2. Have you ever experienced anger? How did you handle the anger?

   _____

   _____

   _____

3. Have you ever experienced fury? How did you handle the fury?

   _____

   _____

   _____

4. What can you do to make sure that your anger does not escalate into fury?

   _____

   _____

   _____

RAGE!

Have you ever been so angry that you lost your ability to think clearly? You did not really know what to do? Were you speechless and was your mind was racing in many directions? Did you feel as if your emotions were rising at a furious rate and you could actually feel your temperature rising, too? Did you feel immobilized? Did you stare, squint, or glare? Did your heart rate and breathing increase? IF THIS HAS EVER HAPPENED TO YOU, YOU WERE AT THE BRINK OF **RAGE**.

Webster's Collegiate Dictionary describes rage as "violent and uncontrollable anger; a fit of violent wrath; insanity; an intense feeling with violent action; to be in tumult and to prevail uncontrollably."

Let's look at some of the words that are connected to rage.

- Violent ___
- Uncontrollable ___
- Anger ___
- Wrath ___
- Insanity ___
- Tumult ___

Place a check mark next to any of these emotions that you feel you have experienced. Now, in the space provided below, choose at least four of these words to look up in the dictionary. Write a definition for the four words you choose on the lines provided.

Violent: _____

Uncontrollable: _____

Anger: _____

Wrath: _____

Insanity: _____

Tumult: _____

Have you ever experienced these emotions? What happened?

_____

_____

_____

_____

Have you experienced someone feeling these emotions toward you? Describe what happened?

_____

_____

_____

_____

Are these emotions you like to be associated with? Why or why not?

_____

_____

_____

How can you avoid feeling these types of emotions?

_____

_____

_____

_____

DEALING WITH RAGE!

The day of the big school science fair had finally arrived, and Sandy was both nervous and excited. She had been up half the night finishing her Mount Helena volcano model and couldn't wait to show it off at the science fair. She hoped to win first prize! If she did, her parents had promised to give her a special present.

As Sandy was setting up her volcano, she noticed her friend Brian's project on the table next to hers. Weeks ago, Brian had asked Sandy for her help in creating a scale model of the solar system, and Sandy had been glad to share her expertise. Brian never told her he was going to enter the solar system in the science fair! Sandy had helped Brian make his solar system beautiful and very unique and showed him how to make it rotate. When the time came for the judges to give the awards, Brian got the blue first place ribbon. Sandy felt crushed.

Sandy thought to herself, "But I worked so hard on my project, and Brian betrayed me by letting me work hard to make his project so good. He didn't even tell me that he was going to enter it into the competition!"

The more she thought about it, the angrier she got. Her heart began beating faster and faster, and she could feel the blood rushing to her face. Suddenly, she couldn't help herself: Sandy marched over to Brian's table, grabbed his solar system, and threw it across the room. When it landed, all of the planets shattered into pieces. Sandy looked up to see the astonished looks on the faces of the teachers and students. She also saw that Brian had begun to cry.

ACTIVITY 1:

Focus on the emotions that Sandy felt when she saw Brian's science fair project. List some of the words that come to your mind. Here are a few to get you started: betrayal and confusion.

_____

_____

_____

_____

_____

ACTIVITY 2:

What do you think Sandy may have looked or acted like when she grabbed Brian's solar system?

_____

_____

_____

_____

_____

What do you think Brian may have looked or acted like when Andy broke his solar system?

_____

_____

_____

_____

What would have been a better way for Sandy to handle this situation?

_____

_____

_____

_____

Is Sandy or Brian at fault in this situation? Why do you feel this way?

_____

_____

_____

_____

_____

_____

_____

_____

_____

WARNING SIGNS OF VIOLENCE!

One of the most important things that you can learn about non-violence is how to recognize signs of potential violence. In this lesson, you will learn the warning signs of violence and ways that you can intervene.

STAGES	WARNING SIGNS	WHAT TO DO TO HELP
ANXIETY	Sighing, fidgeting, nervousness, frowning, rapid breathing, rubbing hands or head, inability to sit, talking louder and faster	Listen and provide non-judgmental feedback. Speak quietly and calmly using a non-threatening position. Be reassuring and comforting.
STRESS	Disruptive behaviors such as disobeying rules, talking loud and out of order, refusing to cooperate, interrupting activities and conversations, drawing negative attention to self and others	Try to provide assistance if possible. Use body language to provide reassurance and comfort. Speak slowly and softly. Redirect focus and conversation to positivity.
DEFENSIVENESS	Arguing and complaining, refusal to listen to reason or allow others to talk, animated facial expressions and body language, Aggressive and threatening body position, use of profanity	Use lower voice volume and tone. Speak slower and softer. Respond by repeating what is being said in a calm and reflective manner to show that you are listening without conflict.
VIOLENCE TO SELF OR OTHERS	Hitting, pushing, slapping, biting, throwing objects, loss of control	Use safe restraint, move away to safety, use safe defense method.
DE-ESCALATION	Crying, non-verbal venting, sullen and broken body positioning.	Encourage understanding about the conflict and its effects on self and others.

DE-ESCALATION SKILLS

When you are angry or upset, it is very easy to move, act, or react before you really think. We must learn how to slow ourselves down so that we can be in control of our own emotions and circumstances. Here are some ways to slow yourself down when you are feeling angry or upset.

1. Take ten deep breaths and honestly consider a peaceful solution.

2. Use controlled breathing: breathe in slowly, hold your breath, and breathe out slowly.

3. Count to twenty-five slowly or quote something silently.

4. Lower the level and volume of your voice; change the tone of your voice.

5. Change where you are standing: make sure you are not standing directly face-to-face with the person you are having the conflict with.

6. Stop talking and begin listening. There may be a chance for resolution.

7. Walk away from the conflict if the situation gets worse.

8. **Understand that when violence occurs, even the winner loses.**

INDIVIDUAL OR FAMILY ASSIGNMENT TO HELP MANAGE ANGER AND CONFLICT

For five days, tally all of the times you use these de-escalation techniques.

DE-ESCALATION TECHNIQUE	Mon	Tues	Weds	Thurs	Fri.
Controlled breathing or deep breaths.					
Counting or quoting silently.					
Lowering your voice tone or volume.					
Changing where you are standing.					
Listening and seeking resolution to conflict.					
Walking away from conflict.					

What did you learn from using de-escalation techniques? Did they work for you? When?

_____

_____

_____

_____

_____

HOW TO RESOLVE CONFLICTS
CONFLICT RESOLUTION

It is important to know that you can stop conflict before it starts. These are the things you need to learn and remember when facing conflict.

STOP. When you lose control of your temper, you will make the conflict worse. It is up to you to think about the consequence of responding to a situation that will potentially bring conflict. One good way to remember this is to say, "I choose my own battles. Is this the battle I need to fight? Am I ready to pay the cost for this battle?"

SAY. Express what you feel is the problem. Many people have serious conflicts over misunderstandings. If you clearly state what you are feeling, there is a better chance that the other person will understand what you are thinking and feeling. A clear solution may be just a conversation away.

UNDERSTAND. Clearly understand what is causing the disagreement. If you can focus on what the problem is and not who you are having the problem with, then it is much easier to resolve the conflict. When people feel that they are being attacked personally, tempers tend to flare. People sometimes forget why they are fighting because they become more focused on whom they are fighting!

RESOLVE. What do you want? If you really understand what you are looking for in any situation, it is so much easier to achieve it. Be realistic. Is the person that you are having the conflict with able to give you what you want? If not, you are fighting a losing battle. If the person can give you what you want, you will have a better chance of receiving what you want through a peaceful resolution of the conflict.

REMEMBER: *WHEN VIOLENCE TAKES PLACE, EVEN THE WINNER LOSES!*

HOW TO WORK OUT CONFLICTS
(K – 1st grade)

Draw pictures to show each of these steps to working out conflict.

STOP before you lose control.	SAY what you feel is the problem.
LISTEN to the other person's feelings.	THINK of what both of you want.

HOW TO WORK OUT CONFLICTS

(3 – 6 grades)

Below are steps that you can take to try to avoid conflict. Think about a situation that caused conflict between you and someone else. How could you have applied these steps to your situation?

STOP before you lose control of your temper and make the conflict worse.

_____

_____

_____

_____

SAY what you feel is the problem. What is causing the disagreement? What do you want in the situation?

_____

_____

_____

_____

LISTEN to the other person's ideas and feelings.

_____

_____

_____

_____

_____

THINK of solutions that will satisfy both of you.

_____

_____

_____

_____

What do you think the result of your conflict would have been if you had applied these steps?

_____

_____

_____

_____

_____

_____

HOW TO WORK OUT CONFLICTS
CONFLICT RESOLUTION (Intermediate)

It is important to know that you can stop conflict before it starts. These are the things you need to learn and remember when facing conflict.

STOP. Know that you are in control of you and never give that up to any person or situation. Always ask yourself the question, "What will this cost me? Am I willing to pay that price, and is it worth it?" Remember, when it comes to violence or crime, even the winner becomes a loser within the justice system…forever.

SAY. If you have a problem about something or with someone, think it through several times and then express it if you still find that it's worth addressing at all. Find the right time to clearly state what you are feeling with open ear to hear and heart to feel the response. Remember the goal is to create greater understanding and respect for both viewpoints.

UNDERSTAND. Clearly understand what is causing the disagreement. If you can focus on what the problem is, and not whom you are having the problem with, then it is much easier to resolve the conflict. When people feel that they are being attacked personally, tempers flare and people forget why they are fighting and become more focused on whom they are fighting! In war, both sides suffer causalities.

RESOLVE. What do you want? If you really understand what you are looking for in any situation, it is so much easier to achieve it. Be realistic. Is the person that you are having the conflict with able to give you what you want? If not, you are fighting a losing battle. If the person can give you what you want, you will have a better chance of receiving what you want through a peaceful resolution of the conflict.

WHERE THERE IS VIOLENCE, EVEN THE WINNER LOSES!

WHAT DO YOU THINK ABOUT WHAT YOU THINK?

For every stressful situation or conflict that comes our way, we need to understand that we do not just respond automatically without thinking. Most people believe that they do this:

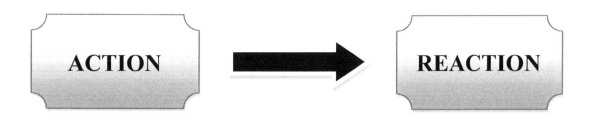

Do you believe that you handle most of your situations this way? Explain why you believe this.

_____

_____

_____

_____

_____

Now consider that you actually complete three steps when you are faced with conflict, not two in your thought process:

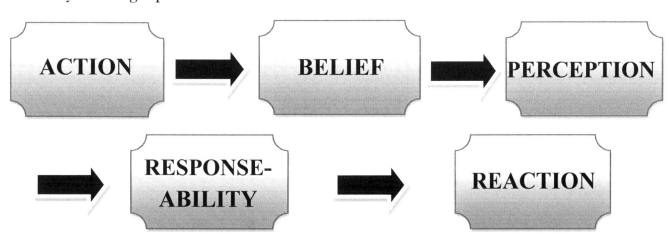

What you **believe** about a situation, or a person, can directly affect your perception of what has taken place. Explain this statement.

_____

_____

_____

_____

Consider the way you handle most of your situations? Can you see how your perception of your situations possibly affected your responses? Give an example using an event in your own life.

_____

_____

_____

_____

Why is what you believe about a situation so important? Has there ever been a situation that you believed was one way, and later you found out that what you believed was completely incorrect? Tell about that situation and how you felt before and after you found out the truth.

_____

_____

_____

_____

_____

RESOLVE.

HOW TO HANDLE YOUR EMOTIONS

We all experience a wide range of emotions in our lives. Usually, that's a good thing, but sometimes, we have difficulty controlling our emotions, even to the point of letting our emotions control our behavior. Usually, that's <u>not</u> such a good thing. Here are some helpful suggestions for handling your emotions.

- **Be honest with yourself.**

- **Talk to somebody about your feelings.**

- **Don't ignore your emotions; they are telling you something.**

- **If you are having an unpleasant feeling, think of something you can do that will help, and then do it.**

- **Find positive ways that are not hurtful to others to express anger.**

- **Remember, whatever you are feeling, you're not alone.**

- **Try not to get overwhelmed; things usually improve.**

- **If you do get overwhelmed—<u>ask for help.</u>**

FAMILY ASSIGNMENTS
FOR ANGER

Take time for the family to sit and watch a television show together. Try to identify situations where anger is expressed. Talk about when the characters are angry and what could have been done to avoid creating situations that produce anger. Write about what you found and your solutions.

_____

_____

_____

_____

_____

Search newspapers and magazines to find articles that talk about people who are having conflicts. Discuss the conflicts: how did they begin; what caused them to escalate; and how could these conflicts be avoided? Write about what you found and the solutions you would recommend.

_____

_____

_____

_____

FIND A PEACEFUL SOLUTION (K – 1st grade)

Go through the maze moving from the angry Lil VMan to the peaceful Lil VMan.

HOW TO PREVENT FIGHTS

Conflict is a normal part of life. We all have occasional conflicts, even with people we love. But we shouldn't let little conflicts turn into fights, especially violent ones. Here are some rules for keeping conflicts from getting out of control.

• Tell the other person what's bothering you, but do it nicely.

• Don't let your emotions take control.

• Listen to the other person.

• Try to understand how the other person is feeling.

• No name-calling or insults.

• No hitting.

• Don't yell or raise your voice.

• Look for a compromise.

If all else fails, ask somebody else for help!

LITTLE PEOPLE, BIG DECISIONS

HATE

LOVE

BULLYING

FORGIVE

VICTORY OVER VIOLENCE

THE NEGATIVE ENERGY NETWORK

This story begins in a swamp, which lead to the Great Ocean and was fed by a big lake. All of the animals needed water to live, so they had to venture past the swamp to get to the lake.

However, there came a time when the existence of the animals was threatened because they could not drink, bathe, or cross the swamp to get to the river without facing great danger. The Negative Energy Plant had created giant alligators to live in the swamp. When the alligators had too many babies, the swamp became over populated with alligators. Other dangerous residents in the swamp were ocean piranha and a giant crocodile named Big Croc. Big Croc, the piranhas, and the mean alligators would eat any animal they could catch in the water. The swamp soon lost all balance and peace.

Big Croc became the Commander-in-Chief of the Negative Energy Plant Network. The Field General was Al-e-gator and Master Puree was leader of the Big Teeth Piranha Gang.

Since the alligators were the size of a sports car, they could be easily seen and avoided by the other animals while they were on land. However, all of the animals were in danger of being eaten if ever caught crossing the swamp.

Every day at dusk, all of the alligators would go into the shallow swamp water to prevent the animals from crossing the swamp to reach the big lake where they could drink and bathe. Once the alligators were in swamp water, they were hidden.

All of the animals knew about the danger. They told stories of the Great Ocean and the schools of fish who were beautiful to the eye, but deadly if approached. These were the piranhas. They

looked like most fish, but their rows and rows of sharp teeth could rip meat, and these fish were always hungry. There were thousands of them! No animal or man, big or small, could survive a battle with the piranha.

The animals realized that something had to be done to combat the Negative Energy Plant Network (NEPN), so an animal network meeting was called. They launched a campaign to create a safe environment for all. They named their campaign the "Drain the Swamp by Any Means Necessary" campaign. They called upon the famed community organizer, Lil VMan, and the V-Crew to carry out their campaign.

Tim-V Turtle was a member of the V-Crew. Although Tim-V was a slow thinker and mover, he still had very good ideas. He often used the wisdom that he gained from listening to his elders and relatives who lived as long as one hundred years. This gave him wisdom. The other animals gained great respect for Tim-V Turtle, despite the fact that he was very slow.

Early in the morning, all the animals, birds, and insects gathered on a shore of the swamp opposite of the one where the alligators were sleeping. Tim-V Turtle had devised a plan to have all of the animals, fowl, and insects drink the shallow swamp water until the swamp was drained. He explained, "If we drain the swamp, we will be free of our fears and the threats of the alligators".

All of the animals remembered their pledge to "Hold Up Your Own End", and were excited about working together to help themselves and others. Each one pledged to take responsibility for their future by giving their best effort to the plan. Even though the insects knew that they could not drink as much water as the larger animals, they still wanted to do what they could do to help. Everyone was important.

Dedicated to completing their goal, they had worked all morning and afternoon, before the alligators woke up to take their evening swim in the swamp. The animals worked so well together that some of them forgot that what they were doing actually involved a great amount of risk. Some of the animals began to get careless and playful, and they begin to splash in the water that they were trying to drain.

To the dismay of all of the animals, the sound of the splashing soon woke up the alligators. Even worse, the splashing caught the attention of the very one that everyone was most afraid of: Big Croc!

The legend of Big Croc was known throughout the swamplands. Very few animals had seen Big Croc face-to-face and lived to tell about it. There were reports from time to time that some of the animals had seen his one eye moving silently under the swamp water.

Some of the animals who lived in the trees said Big Croc was as large as a school bus! He spent all of his time creating negative energy, attitudes, and behaviors such as hate, harm, anger, revenge, depression, and hopelessness. He made swamp life miserable.

As Big Croc entered the swamp, all of the animals, birds, and even the insects scattered in every direction. The wonderful project to drain the swamp came to an abrupt halt.

As the evening came upon the swamp and all of the animals had retreated to the safety of their own homes, a great lesson rested upon the minds of each and every creature that evening, as they realized that losing focus had caused them to miss the opportunity to complete their goal. They learned a valuable lesson that day:

"YOU HAVE TO STAY FOCUSED ON THE GOAL TO BE SUCCESSFUL IN WHAT YOU ARE TRYING TO ACHIEVE!"

TRY TO PRACTICE "ANWOT":

A	=	A
N	=	NEW
W	=	WAY
O	=	OF
T	=	THINKING

SO THAT YOU CAN LEARN TO

"H.U.Y.O.E."

HOLD UP YOUR OWN END!

WHAT HAPPENED

IN THE "NEGATIVE ENERGY" STORY?

CAN YOU PICTURE THE STORY?

(K – 1st grade - Sequencing Skills)

Directions: In each box, draw a picture of what happened in the story. In box 1, show what happened firstly. In box 2, show what happened secondly. In box 3, show what happened thirdly, and in box 4, show what was the last thing that happened in the story.

| WHAT HAPPENED <u>FIRST</u> IN THE STORY? | 1 |

WHAT HAPPENED SECOND IN THE STORY?

2

WHAT HAPPENED THIRD IN THE STORY?

3

HOW DID THE STORY END?

WHAT HAPPENED <u>LAST</u> IN THE STORY?	4

WHAT DID YOU LEARN FROM THE STORY?	5

THE STORY

(grades 3-6)

Do you know the difference between **Retelling** and **Summarizing** a story? This will help you.

Retelling: Tell the story, repeating the details and words exactly as they are in the story. (Quote dialogue when you can.)

Summarizing: Briefly tell the story, giving the main points using your own words, not words from the story.

RETELL THE STORY OF "THE NEGATIVE ENERGY NETWORK".

_____

_____

_____

_____

_____

SUMMARIZE THE STORY OF "THE NEGATIVE ENERGY NETWORK".

_____

_____

_____

_____

_____

_____

HOW WELL DID YOU READ?

Reading Comprehension Activity
(Intermediate)

In your own words, explain what the problem is in the story.

_____

_____

_____

_____

_____

_____

How did the characters in this story respond to the problem? Was this the best solution?

_____

_____

_____

Now practice your writing skills by RETELLING and SUMMARIZING the story.

Remember that when you *retell* a story, you use the characters' actual dialogue and use

specific details exactly as they were stated in the story. When you *summarize* a story, you

simply paraphrase or describe events in the story in your own words.

RETELL the story of the Negative Energy Network.

_____

_____

_____

_____

SUMMARIZE the story of the Negative Energy Network.

DEFEATING NEGATIVE ENERGY

```
                    B E X
                O I F G A F C L X
                I Q T E F A P I O P R W W
            H Y O K Z X W F M W M O B Q N O C
            Q T A G J N W B F A D P C K C C M T W
          N Q L A H E W G I Y W A L V W C P W C E J
          B A W E R C M S K Y S N E S F S T C N J S
        D R H D W W       Z R Y B T       C L Z P A A
        A W S R W V       Y V H V E       I P J X S M
      Z I O C A C Z O K P I O L N A A V S P E A Z L Y C
      Z O H W I N F Y A N M Y F Y R L F P Z K E D A O J
      V B P H N I E G Y O V C F N F O Z E B Z I M M Y H
    M B U X P E X X H S I N I F E I L Z S B B M I Q H J
    B N F M Z I S U O V G P R D I F E A R B F I G N N S Q
    M C C C X A T S P L A S H F P F X D H P T L W A L W C
    B R I M     S Q P U U Q L A M X I W Y T I     L Q T T
    Z W Q H       V C U X S Q Y F K Y Q E B       Q K H O
    S W S I B       I M G R B Q K B H D N       M R B N E
      L P T O T                             L O V Y P
      H A F S W L                           D W Z V A D
        R O Z Z N T Z P V E Q D J E J F T G L A S
        N B G O E U C E G W P U Q L U E W B G C P
        R D K D F H J Q M P C Y D N H L H K B
          J F T G O W U Q V O U U D X C R I
            Y Z P F R Q P H V R D E N
              E H B R O L T Q S
                  C S X
```

- NETWORK
- SWAMP
- SPLASH
- FINISH
- CREW
- FEAR
- COMPLETE
- COMMITTED
- DRAIN
- HOPE
- GOALS
- ANIMALS

DEFEATING NEGATIVE ENERGY
ANSWER KEY

```
                        B E X
                    O I F G A F C L X
                  I Q T E F A P I O P R W W
                H Y O K Z X W F M W O B Q N O C
              Q T A G J N W B F A D P C K C C M T W
              N Q L A H E W G I Y W A L V W C P W C E J
              B A W E R C M S K Y S N E S F S T C N J S
            D R H D W W         Z R Y B T     C L Z P A A
            A W S R W V         Y V H V E     I P J X S M
        Z I O C A C Z O K P I O L N A A V S P E A Z L Y C
        Z O H W I N F Y A N M Y F Y R L F P Z K E D A O J
        V B P H N I E G Y O V C F N F O Z E B Z I M M Y H
      M B U X P E X X H S I N I F E I L Z X S B B M I Q H J
      B N F M Z I S U O V G P R D I F E A R B F I G N N S Q
      M C C C X A T S P L A S H F P F X D H P T L W A L W C
        B R I M     S Q P U U Q L A M X I W Y T I   L Q T T
        Z W Q H     V C U X S Q Y F K Y Q E B   Q K H O
      S W S I B     I M G R B Q K B H D N     M R B N E
        L P T O T                       L O V Y P
        H A F S W L                 D W Z V A D
          R O Z Z N T Z P V E Q D J E J F T G L A S
          N B G O E U C E G W P U Q L U E W B G C P
            R D K D F H J Q M P C Y D N H L H K B
            J F T G O W U Q V O U U D X C R I
              Y Z P F R Q P H V R D E N
                  E H B R O L T Q S
                    C S X
```

- NETWORK
- SWAMP
- SPLASH
- FINISH

- CREW
- FEAR
- COMPLETE
- COMMITTED

- DRAIN
- HOPE
- GOALS
- ANIMALS

DEFEATING NEGATIVE ENERGY (K-2)

Turn the negative thoughts into positive thoughts by matching them.

1. FEAR   a. SUCCESS

2. HAPPY   b. LISTEN

3. WEAK   c. CONFIDENT

4. MEAN   d. KIND

5. FAILURE   e. COMPLETE

6. INCOMPLETE   f. SAD

7. INSECURE   g. FAST

8. SLOW   h. STRONG

9. DANGEROUS   i. COURAGE

10. IGNORE   j. SAFE

DEFEATING NEGATIVE ENERGY (K-2)
ANSWER KEY

1. _i_ FEAR   a. SUCCESS

2. _f_ HAPPY   b. LISTEN

3. _h_ WEAK   c. CONFIDENT

4. _d_ MEAN   d. KIND

5. _a_ FAILURE   e. COMPLETE

6. _e_ INCOMPLETE   f. SAD

7. _c_ INSECURE   g. FAST

8. _g_ SLOW   h. STRONG

9. _j_ DANGEROUS   i. COURAGE

10. _b_ IGNORE   j. SAFE

THE LIL VMAN PLEDGE AGAINST VIOLENCE

WILL YOU MAKE THIS PLEDGE AGAINST VIOLENCE?

I claim victory over violence in my life.
I claim victory over violence in my home and community.
I claim victory over violence in my school.
I pledge to team up with other people who claim non-violence,

**KNOWING THAT EVEN ONE PERSON
CAN MAKE A DIFFERENCE!**

MEETING WITH THE V-CREW (INTERMEDIATE)

VISUAL PERCEPTION PUZZLE

Find your way through the maze away from Big Croc to meet with the V-Crew.

MEETING WITH THE V-CREW (INTERMEDIATE)
VISUAL PERCEPTION PUZZLE ANSWER KEY

WHERE DO WE GO FROM HERE?

Whose Job is it?

This is a story about four people named Everybody, Somebody, Anybody, and Nobody.

Now, there was an important job to be done, and Everybody was asked to do it. Everybody was sure Somebody would do it. Anybody could have done it, but Nobody did it.

Now, Somebody got angry about that, because it was Everybody's job. Everybody thought that Anybody could have done it, but Nobody realized that Everybody wouldn't do it.

So, it ended up that Everybody blamed Somebody when Nobody did what Anybody could have done.

(Source unknown)

"FOR ALSO KNOWLEDGE ITSELF
IS POWER"
Sir Francis Bacon

In every aspect of violence, there is an element of power, whether it be the struggle for power, the absence of power, or the deviant behavior that arises from the abuse of power.

It has also been evidenced that the presence of increased self-esteem reduces the occurrence of violence. Empowering children and young adults and elevating their self-esteem arise as viable components in the possible solution to the increase in violence in youth culture.

Hence, this chapter is dedicated to the purpose of T.I.M.E: Training, Information, Motivation, and Education. The research, articles, and information presented are divided into three sections: (1) Information and Empowerment for Children and Youth, (2) Information and Empowerment for Parents and Teachers, and (3) Lesson Plans.

Resource locations, references, and all websites are noted in the bibliography. Additional information and research information may be obtained from the noted authors and their works.

INFORMATION AND EMPOWERMENT RESOURCES FOR CHILDREN AND YOUTH

Dealing with Bullies

Bullying is a big problem. It can make kids feel hurt, scared, sick, lonely, embarrassed, and <u>sad</u>. Bullies might hit, kick, or push to hurt people, or use words to call names, threaten, tease, or scare them. A bully might say mean things about someone, grab a kid's stuff, make fun of someone, or leave a kid out of the group on purpose. Some bullies threaten people or try to make them do things they don't want to do.

Bullying Is a Big Deal

Bullying is a big problem that affects lots of kids. Three-quarters of all kids say they have been bullied or teased. Being bullied can make kids feel really bad. The stress of dealing with bullies can make kids feel sick.

Bullying can make kids not want to play outside or go to school. It's hard to keep your mind on schoolwork when you're worried about how you're going to deal with the bully near your locker. Bullying bothers everyone — and not just the kids who are getting picked on. Bullying can make school a place of fear and can lead to more violence and more stress for everyone.

Why Do Bullies Act That Way?

Some bullies are looking for attention. They might think bullying is a way to be popular or to get what they want. Most bullies are trying to make themselves feel more important. When they pick on someone else, it can make them feel big and powerful.

Some bullies come from <u>families where everyone is angry and shouting</u> all the time. They may think that being angry, calling names, and pushing people around is a normal way to act. Some bullies are copying what they've seen someone else do. Some have been bullied themselves.

Sometimes bullies know that what they are doing or saying hurts other people. But other bullies may not really know how hurtful their actions can be. Most bullies don't understand or care about the feelings of others.

Bullies often pick on someone they think they can have power over. They might pick on kids who get upset easily or who have trouble sticking up for themselves. Getting a big reaction out of someone can make bullies feel like they have the power they want. Sometimes bullies pick on someone who is smarter than they are or different from them in some way. Sometimes bullies just pick on a kid for no reason at all.

Gemma told her mom that this one kid was picking on her for having red hair and freckles. She wanted to be like the other kids but she couldn't change those things about herself. Finally, Gemma made friends at her local swimming pool. with a girl who wished she had red hair like Gemma's. The two girls became great friends, and she learned to ignore the mean girl's taunts at school.

Bullying: How to Handle It

So now you know that bullying is a big problem that affects a lot of kids, but what do you do if someone is bullying you? Our advice falls into two categories: preventing a run-in with the bully, and what to do if you end up face-to-face with the bully.

Preventing a Run-In With a Bully

Don't give the bully a chance. As much as you can, avoid the bully. You can't go into hiding or skip class, of course. But if you can take a different route and avoid him or her, do so.

Stand tall and be brave. When you're scared of another person, you're probably not feeling your bravest. But sometimes just acting brave is enough to stop a bully. How does a brave person look and act? Stand tall and you'll send the message: "Don't mess with me." It's easier to feel brave when you feel good about yourself. (See the next tip!)

Feel good about you. Nobody's perfect, but what can you do to look and feel your best? Maybe you'd like to be more fit. If so, maybe you'll decide to get more exercise, watch less TV, and eat healthier snacks. Or maybe you feel you look best when you shower in the morning before school. If so, you could decide to get up a little earlier so you can be clean and refreshed for the school day.

Get a buddy (and be a buddy). Two is better than one if you're trying to avoid being bullied. Make a plan to walk with a friend or two on the way to school or recess or lunch or wherever you think you might meet the bully. Offer to do the same if a friend is having bully trouble. Get involved if you see bullying going on in your school — tell an adult, stick up for the kid being bullied, and tell the bully to stop.

If The Bully Says or Does Something to You

Ignore the bully. If you can, try your best to ignore the bully's threats. Pretend you don't hear them and walk away quickly to a place of safety. Bullies want a big reaction to their teasing and meanness. Acting as if you don't notice and don't care is like giving no reaction at all, and this just might stop a bully's behavior.

Stand up for yourself. Pretend to feel really brave and confident. Tell the bully "No! Stop it!" in a loud voice. Then walk away, or run if you have to. Kids also can stand up for each other by telling a bully to stop teasing or scaring someone else, and then walk away together. If a bully wants you to do something that you don't want to do — say "no!" and walk away. If you do what a bully says to do, they will likely keep bullying you. Bullies tend to bully kids who don't stick up for themselves.

Don't bully back. Don't hit, kick, or push back to deal with someone bullying you or your friends. Fighting back just satisfies a bully and it's dangerous, too, because someone could get hurt. You're also likely to get in trouble. It's best to stay with others, stay safe, and get help from an adult.

Don't show your feelings. Plan ahead. How can you stop yourself from getting angry or showing you're upset? Try distracting yourself (counting backwards from one hundred, spelling the word 'turtle' backwards, etc.) to keep your mind occupied until you are out of the situation and somewhere safe where you can show your feelings.

Tell an adult. If you are being bullied, it's very important to tell an adult. Find someone you trust and go and tell them what is happening to you. Teachers, principals, parents, and lunchroom helpers at school can all help to stop bullying. Sometimes bullies stop as soon as a teacher finds out because they're afraid that they will be punished by parents. This is not tattling on someone who has done something small — bullying is wrong and it helps if everyone who gets bullied or sees someone being bullied speaks up.

What Happens to Bullies?

In the end, most bullies wind up in trouble. If they keep acting mean and hurtful, sooner or later they may have only a few friends left — usually other kids who are just like them. The power they wanted slips away fast. Other kids move on and leave bullies behind.

Luis lived in fear of Brian — every day he would give his lunch money to Brian, but he still beat him up. He said that if Luis ever told anyone, he would beat him up in front of all the other kids in his class. Luis even cried one day, and another girl told everyone that he was a baby and had been crying. Luis was embarrassed and felt so bad about himself and about school. Finally, Brian got caught threatening Luis, and they were both sent to the school counselor. Brian got in a lot of trouble at home. Over time, Brian learned how to make friends and ask his parents for lunch money. Luis never wanted to be friends with Brian, but he did learn to act strong and more confident around him.

Some kids who bully blame others. But every kid has a choice about how to act. Some kids who bully realize that they don't get the respect they want by threatening others. They may have thought that bullying would make them popular, but they soon find out that other kids just think of them as trouble-making losers.

The good news is that kids who are bullies can learn to change their behavior. Teachers, counselors, and parents can help. So can watching kids who treat others fairly and with respect. Bullies can change if they learn to use their power in positive ways. In the end, whether bullies decide to change their ways is up to them. Some bullies turn into great kids. Some bullies never learn.

But no one needs to put up with a bully's behavior. If you or someone you know is bothered by a bully, talk to someone you trust. Everyone has the right to feel safe, and being bullied makes people feel unsafe. Tell someone about it and keep telling until something is done.

Reviewed by: Michelle New, PhD
Date reviewed: July 2007
© 1995- 2010 . The Nemours Foundation/KidsHealth®. Reprinted with permission.

Dealing With Peer Pressure

"Come on! ALL of us are cutting math. Who wants to go take that quiz? We're going to take a walk and get lunch instead. Let's go!" says the coolest kid in your class. Do you do what you know is right and go to math class, quiz and all? Or do you give in and go with them?

As you grow older, you'll be faced with some challenging decisions. Some don't have a clear right or wrong answer — like should you play soccer or field hockey? Other decisions involve serious moral questions, like whether to cut class, try <u>cigarettes</u>, or lie to your parents.

Making decisions on your own is hard enough, but when other people get involved and try to pressure you one way or another, it can be even harder. People who are your age, like your classmates, are called peers. When they try to influence how you act, to get you to do something, it's called **peer pressure**. It's something everyone has to deal with — even adults. Let's talk about how to handle it.

Defining Peer Pressure

Peers influence your life, even if you don't realize it, just by spending time with you. You learn from them, and they learn from you. It's only human nature to listen to and learn from other people in your age group.

Peers can have a positive influence on each other. Maybe another student in your science class taught you an easy way to remember the planets in the solar system, or someone on the soccer team taught you a cool trick with the ball. You might admire a friend who is always a good sport and try to be more like him or her. Maybe you got others excited about your new favorite book, and now everyone's reading it. These are examples of how peers positively influence each other every day.

Sometimes peers influence each other in negative ways. For example, a few kids in school might try to get you to cut class with them, your soccer friend might try to convince you to be mean to another player and never pass her the ball, or a kid in the neighborhood might want you to <u>shoplift</u> with him.

Why Do People Give in to Peer Pressure?

Some kids give in to peer pressure because they want to be liked, to fit in, or because they worry that other kids might make fun of them if they don't go along with the group. Others go along because they are curious to try something new that others are doing. The idea that "everyone's doing it" can influence some kids to leave their better judgment, or their common sense, behind.

Walking Away From Peer Pressure

It is tough to be the only one who says "no" to peer pressure, but you can do it. Paying attention to your own feelings and beliefs about what is right and wrong can help you know the right thing to do. Inner strength and self-confidence can help you stand firm, walk away, and resist doing something when you know better.

It can really help to have at least one other peer, or friend, who is willing to say "no," too. This takes a lot of the power out of peer pressure and makes it much easier to resist. It's great to have friends with values similar to yours who will back you up when you don't want to do something.

You've probably had a parent or teacher advise you to "choose your friends wisely." Peer pressure is a big reason why they say this. If you choose friends who don't use drugs, cut class, smoke cigarettes, or lie to their parents, then you probably won't do these things either, even if other kids do. Try to help a friend who's having trouble resisting peer pressure. It can be powerful for one kid to join another by simply saying, "I'm with you — let's go."

Even if you're faced with peer pressure while you're alone, there are still things you can do. You can simply stay away from peers who pressure you to do stuff you know is wrong. You can tell them "no" and walk away. Better yet, find other friends and classmates to pal around with.

If you continue to face peer pressure and you're finding it difficult to handle, talk to someone you trust. Don't feel guilty if you've made a mistake or two. Talking to a parent, teacher, or school counselor can help you feel much better and prepare you for the next time you face peer pressure.

Powerful, Positive Peer Pressure

Peer pressure is not always a bad thing. For example, positive peer pressure can be used to pressure bullies into acting better toward other kids. If enough kids get together, peers can pressure each other into doing what's right!

Reviewed by: Mary L. Gavin, MD
Date reviewed: June 2010
Originally reviewed by: Kevin J. Took, MD

How Cliques Make Kids Feel Left Out

At recess one day, Madison's teacher found her sitting alone at lunch, looking sad and upset. She could barely bite the peanut butter sandwich that she usually couldn't wait to eat. "What's the matter, Madison?" the teacher asked.

Later that afternoon, Trey was standing alone by the basketball court after school. Trey's mom asked him why he didn't go play with Zack and Steve, who were shooting hoops. He told his mom he just didn't feel like it, so they walked home.

But the truth was, Trey and Madison were facing the same problem: They both felt left out, and their feelings were hurt.

Madison was so sad that she didn't want to eat, and Trey was so mad that when he got home he slammed his bedroom door. Kids who were their friends yesterday weren't their friends today. What happened?

What Are Cliques?

Cliques are groups of friends, but not all groups of friends are cliques. The thing that makes a group a **clique** (say: **klik**) is that they leave some kids out on purpose. Usually one or two popular kids control who gets to be in the clique and who gets left out. Kids may act much differently than they did before they were part of the clique.

Everyone feels left out by friends once in a while. Friends are people just like us — they make mistakes and usually we can forgive them (after all, we make mistakes too!). Sometimes friends fight and make up again.

But sometimes kids form groups that they won't let other kids belong to. A clique is a group of kids who hang out together and won't let others join in. Sometimes kids in the clique are mean to kids they think are on the outside.

For instance, Trey and Steve always played basketball after school. But Zack started pushing Trey out of the group, and now even Steve was saying mean stuff to Trey. Same with Madison and Allie. They used to have sleepovers all the time, but now Cleo was hosting the sleepovers and she didn't invite Madison.

Kids might form cliques in elementary school or in middle school. Sometimes cliques are made of kids who share an interest in something, like sports or computer games or music. Sometimes the kids in them want to be popular or want to belong.

Both boys and girls have cliques, though people who study these groups say girl cliques may be worse. Girl cliques are often meaner and more hurtful in the way they treat girls who aren't in the group.

Feeling Left Out

If you are on the outside of a clique, it can hurt your feelings. You might feel very frustrated, angry, or sad and want to cry or say mean things about the people in the clique. You might feel lonely if you're alone at lunch or after school, or even afraid if you feel that someone might pick on you or fight with you. You might be frustrated or upset because you don't know what to do. You might feel down on yourself because the group doesn't want you as a member. You might feel hurt because of the ways other kids keep you out.

Why Do Other Kids Join Cliques?

One of the hard things about cliques is if a person who was your friend joins one and starts treating you differently. Sometimes, the problem starts with an argument between the two of you. But other times you can find yourself on the outside of a clique even if nothing happened.

Sometimes you get left out because you look, act, or dress differently from the other kids. Or just because you're the "new kid" in class. Kids who get into cliques usually want to be popular and feel cool. Sometimes kids think that belonging to a clique will keep them from feeling left out. Some kids feel more powerful when they are mean to other people (like bullies).

Kids in cliques sometimes act differently than they would outside the group. They often go along with what the others are doing, even if they know it's not right — even if it means leaving out a friend. They might feel bad about it, but they can't figure out how to be cool and still be nice to the person who's not in the clique. This is no excuse, though. Plenty of kids manage to be nice to everyone — kids in and outside their closest group of friends — without being part of a clique.

Feeling Trapped in a Clique

Sometimes kids in cliques find that they don't really want to belong to it anymore. They don't want to be bossed around by the rules of the clique, and they don't want to leave others out and hurt people's feelings.

Sometimes they realize they are missing out on being friends with great kids outside of the clique. Some kids realize that they have to give up some freedom and maybe even change the kind of people they are or what kind of music they like or clothes they want to wear.

Even if no one is being mean to you personally, you still might find it annoying if there are cliques you're not welcome to be part of. Or you might be part of a clique, but are getting tired of being bossed around.

As kids get older, they usually outgrow the need to be part of a clique or they are more relaxed about who is "in" and who is "out." For some kids this takes a while. Most cliques have disappeared by the end of high school, making way for more fun and enjoyable friendship groups.

Who Can Help?

Parents, sisters and brothers, other family members, and teachers can help when someone is being left out or treated in a mean way. They might help by giving you advice on how to deal with mean kids. Sometimes they can teach kids that it isn't OK to treat others this way and show them ways to stop kids being mean to other kids.

If you or someone you know is being treated meanly or bullied by members of a clique, telling an adult is important. Adults can also help kids learn to play together, include each other, mend hurt feelings, and repair broken friendships. They can encourage kids to make friends and belong to a group without leaving others out. They can show kids how to be popular by treating everyone with respect and kindness.

What You Can Do

If cliques are upsetting you, what can you do?

- **Find friends.** If you find yourself left out of a certain group, focus on other friends. Hang out with kids who aren't part of a clique. Sometimes this means finding older or younger kids to hang out with, or making friends outside school. Sometimes it means being open to kids who look or act differently than you do.
- **Speak up.** If your group of friends has suddenly turned into a clique, speak up. It's OK to say that you want to invite others to hang out with you, too. Be prepared for the fact

that the clique might go on without you. On the other hand, others might follow your lead and stop acting so clique-y.

- **Invite a friend.** If you're on the outside of a clique and you want to be friends with someone who's in it, invite that person to do something with you. It might help if you can see your friend away from the other clique members. Maybe your mom or dad could arrange to have that friend visit at your house on the weekend. By spending time together, he or she might start realizing how silly it is not to hang out more often. But also be prepared for possible disappointment. Even if you have a great time together, your friend might still slip back into the clique when you're all back at school.

- **Don't take it out on yourself.** Some kids feel they should try to change themselves — and that's OK, too. Maybe you want to get <u>healthy and fit</u> or learn to smile more and be less cranky; — it's great to work on yourself, but do it for you, not for anyone else. If some kids are mean to you because they think you don't fit in, don't let them make decisions about the kind of kid you are going to be. Decide for yourself and then get help to reach your goals. Ask a cool cousin or friend to help you revamp your wardrobe or get a new <u>haircut</u>. But only change yourself if it's something you want to do.

- **Look for friends everywhere.** The most popular and well-liked kids are the ones who are friendly to everyone. Do your best to let everyone feel welcome to talk to you. Look for chances to meet, talk with, and play with plenty of different kids. Is someone sitting alone at lunch? Why not ask her to sit at your table? Or maybe you noticed the kid standing outside the fence while you were playing basketball. It's time to invite him onto the court. Who knows — maybe the two of you will really click (which means to get along really well). Now that's a much better kind of click!

Reviewed by: <u>Michelle New, PhD</u>
Date reviewed: September 2007

The Story on Self-Esteem

You can't touch it, but it affects how you feel. You can't see it, but it's there when you look at yourself in the mirror. You can't hear it, but it's there every time you talk about yourself. What is this important but mysterious thing? It's your self-esteem!

What Is Self-Esteem?

To understand self-esteem, it helps to break the term into two words. Let's take a look at the word **esteem** (say: ess-**teem**) first. Esteem is a fancy word for thinking that someone or something is important or valuing that person or thing. For example, if you really admire your friend's dad because he volunteers at the fire department, it means you hold him in high esteem. And the special trophy for the most valuable player on a team is often called an esteemed trophy. This means the trophy stands for an important accomplishment.

And **self** means, well, yourself! So put the two words together and it's easier to see what self-esteem is. It's how much you value yourself and how important you think you are. It's how you see yourself and how you feel about your achievements.

Self-esteem isn't bragging about how great you are. It's more like quietly knowing that you're worth a lot (priceless, in fact!). It's not about thinking you're perfect — because nobody is — but knowing that you're worthy of being loved and accepted.

Why Self-Esteem Is Important

Self-esteem isn't like a cool pair of sneakers that you'd love to have but don't have to have. A kid needs to have self-esteem. Good self-esteem is important because it helps you to hold your head high and feel proud of yourself and what you can do. It gives you the courage to try new things and the power to believe in yourself. It lets you respect yourself, even when you make mistakes. And when you respect yourself, adults and other kids usually respect you, too.

Having good self-esteem is also the ticket to making good choices about your mind and body. If you think you're important, you'll be less likely to follow the crowd if your friends are doing something dumb or dangerous. If you have good self-esteem, you know that you're smart enough to make your own decisions. You value your safety, your feelings, your health — your whole self! Good self-esteem helps you know that every part of you is worth caring for and protecting.

How Kids Get Self-Esteem

Babies don't see themselves in a good or bad way. They don't think "I'm great!" when they let out a big burp or worry "Oh, no, this diaper makes my legs look weird!" Instead, people around a baby help him or her develop self-esteem. How? By encouraging the baby when he or she learns to crawl, walk, or talk. They often say, "Good job. Good for you!" When people take good care of a baby, that also helps him or her feel lovable and valuable.

As kids get older, they can have a bigger role in developing their self-esteem. Achievements — like getting a good grade on a test, or making the All-Star soccer team — are things kids can be proud of. So are having a good sense of humor or being a good friend.

A kid's family and other people in his or her life — like coaches, teammates, and classmates — also can boost his or her self-esteem. They can help a kid figure out how to do things or notice his or her good qualities. They can believe in the kid and encourage him or her to try again when something doesn't go right the first time. It's all part of kids learning to see themselves in a positive way, to feel proud of what they've done, and to be confident that there's a lot more they can do.

A Little on Low Self-Esteem

Maybe you know kids with low self-esteem who don't think very highly of themselves or seem to criticize themselves too much. Or maybe you have low self-esteem and don't always feel very good about yourself or think you're important.

Sometimes a kid will have low self-esteem if his mother or father doesn't encourage him enough or if there is a lot of yelling at home. Other times, a kid's self-esteem can be hurt in the classroom. A teacher may make a kid feel dumb or perhaps there is a bully who says hurtful things.

For some kids, classes at school can seem so hard that they can't keep up or get the grades they'd hoped for. This can make them feel bad about themselves and hurt their self-esteem. Their self-esteem will improve when a teacher, tutor, or counselor encourages them, is patient, and helps them get back on track with learning. When they start to do well, their self-esteem will skyrocket!

And some kids have good self-esteem but then something happens to change that. For example:

- If a kid moves and doesn't make friends right away at the new school, he or she might start to feel bad.
- Kids whose parents divorce also may find that this can affect self-esteem. They may feel unlovable or to blame for the divorce.
- A kid who feels too fat or too thin may start thinking that means he or she isn't good enough.

- A kid who's dealing with an illness, such as <u>cancer</u>, diabetes, or asthma, might feel different and less confident than before.
- Even going through the body changes of <u>puberty</u> — something that everybody does — can affect a kid's self-esteem.

Boosting Your Self-Esteem

Of course it's OK to have ups and downs in your feelings, but having low self-esteem isn't OK. Feeling like you're not important can make you sad and can keep you from trying new things. It can keep you from making friends or hurt how you do at school.

Having strong self-esteem is also a very big part of growing up. As you get older and face tough decisions — especially under peer pressure — the more self-esteem you have, the better. It's important to know you're worth a lot.

If you think you might have low self-esteem, try talking to an adult you trust about it. He or she may be able to help you come up with some good ideas for building your self-esteem.

In the meantime, here are a few things that you can try to increase your self-esteem:

- **Make a list of the stuff you're good at.** It can be anything from drawing or singing to playing a sport or telling a good joke. If you're having trouble with your list, ask your mom or dad to help you with it. Then add a few things to the list that you'd like to be good at. Your mom or dad can help you plan a way to work on those skills or talents.
- **Give yourself three compliments every day.** Don't just say, "I'm so great." Be specific about something good about yourself, like, "I was a good friend to Jill today" or "I did better on that test than I thought I would." While you're at it, before you go to bed every night, list three things in your day that really made you happy.
- **Remember that your body is your own, no matter what shape, size, or color it is.** If you are worried about your weight or size, you can check with your doctor to make sure that things are OK. Remind yourself of things about your body that are cool, like, "My legs are strong and I can skate really well."
- **Remember that there are things about yourself you can't change.** You should accept and love these things — such as skin color and shoe size — because they are part of you.
- **When you hear negative comments in your head, tell yourself to stop.** When you do this, you take the power away from the voice inside that discourages you.

By focusing on the good things you do and all your great qualities, you learn to love and accept yourself — the main ingredients for strong self-esteem! Even if you've got room for improvement (and who doesn't?), realizing that you're valuable and important helps your self-esteem to shine.

Reviewed by: <u>David V. Sheslow, PhD</u>
November 2008

Taking Charge of Anger

Have you ever lost your temper? Did you yell and scream or want to hit someone? Maybe your little brother got into your room and played with your toys without permission. Or maybe your teacher gave you too much <u>homework</u>. Or maybe a friend borrowed your favorite video game and then broke it. That made you angry!

Everyone gets angry. Maybe you "lose your cool" or "hit the roof." Anger can even be a good thing. When kids are treated unfairly, anger can help them stand up for themselves. The hard part is learning **what to do** with these strong feelings.

What Is Anger?

You have lots of emotions. At different times, you may be happy, <u>sad</u>, or jealous. Anger is just another way we feel. It's perfectly OK to be angry at times — in fact, it's important to get angry sometimes.

But anger must be released in the right way. Otherwise you'll be like a pot of boiling water with the lid left on. If the steam doesn't escape, the water will finally boil over and blow its top! When that happens to you, it's no fun for anyone.

What Makes You Angry?

Many things may make kids angry. You may get angry when something doesn't go your way. Maybe you get mad at yourself when you don't understand your homework or when your team loses an important game. When you have a hard time reaching a goal, you might become frustrated. That frustration can lead to anger.

Kids who <u>tease</u> you or call you names can make you angry. Or you might get angry with your parents if you think one of their rules is unfair. Worst of all is when you are blamed for something you didn't do. But it's also possible to get angry and not even know why.

How Can I Tell When I'm Angry?

There are different ways people feel anger. Usually your body will tell you when you are angry. Are you breathing faster? Is your face bright red? Are your muscles tense and your fists clenched tight? Do you want to break something or hit someone? Anger can make you yell or scream at those around you, even people you like or love.

Some people keep their anger buried deep inside. If you do this, you might get a <u>headache</u> or your stomach might start to hurt. You may just feel crummy about yourself or start to cry. It's not good to hide your anger, so you should find a way to let it out without hurting yourself or others.

How Can I Tell When Someone Else Is Angry?

When someone you know is angry, he or she may stomp away or stop talking to you, or become quiet and withdrawn. Some people scream and try to hit or harm anyone close by. If a person is this angry, you should get away as soon as possible.

Once you are away from the angry person, stop and think. Try to figure out what made that person so angry. Can you make the situation better? How does the other person feel? When the other person has cooled down, try to talk about the problem. Listen to what he or she has to say.

What Should I Do If I Get Angry?

Don't lose control if you get angry. Taking it out on others never solves anything. Instead, admit to yourself that you are angry and try to figure out why. What can **you** do to keep the situation from happening again? If your little sister gets a toy and you don't, it's not OK to break that toy. Maybe you can ask her to share it with you. Or if your science homework is too hard, don't rip up your notebook. Ask your teacher or a parent for help instead.

It helps to <u>talk</u> about your anger with an adult, such as a parent, teacher, or relative. Once you talk about anger, those bad feelings usually start to go away.

Anger Busters

Here are some other things you can do when you start to feel angry:

- talk to a friend you can trust
- count to ten
- get or give a hug
- do jumping jacks or another exercise
- draw a picture of your anger
- play a video game
- run around the outside of the house five times as fast as you can
- sing along with the stereo
- pull weeds in the garden
- think good thoughts (maybe about a fun vacation or your favorite sport)
- take a bike ride, go skateboarding, play basketball — do something active!

Never getting angry is impossible. Instead, remember that how you act when you're angry can make the situation better or worse. **Don't let anger be the boss of you.** Take charge of it!

Reviewed by: D'Arcy Lyness, PhD
Date reviewed: October 2010

Train Your Temper

Everybody gets <u>angry</u> sometimes. Being angry doesn't really solve much — but what people do when they feel angry is important. The goal is to calm yourself down and try to solve whatever problem is bothering you. This is hard for some kids (and adults, too). Instead of calming down, some kids might keep getting more and more upset until they explode like a volcano!

Some kids get angry more often or more easily than some other kids. Their anger might be so strong that the feeling gets out of control and causes them to act in ways that are unacceptable and hurtful. People might say kids like this **have a temper**, which is a term for acting all angry and out of control. When people say that someone has trouble controlling their temper, they usually mean that a kid behaves badly when feeling angry or frustrated.

Some kids might get so angry that they scream at their mom or dad, punch the wall, slam doors, break something, or — worse yet — hit a <u>brother or sister</u>. Kids are allowed to express their feelings, even angry ones, but it's not OK for a kid to do any of those things. Kids don't want to (or mean to) act this way — but sometimes angry feelings can be hard to manage. So what do you do if you're a volcano kind of a kid and your temper is getting you into trouble?

Arf! Try This!

Well, the good news is that kids don't just have to keep making the same mistakes over and over again. You can train your temper the same way you might train a puppy. Huh? That's right, we said a puppy.

If you've ever played with puppies, you know they are sweet but a little out of control. Their tails wag furiously and they might tear apart your sneakers or nip at the mailman's behind. Oh dear, what can you do with your puppy? Training is the answer.

In the same way, you can train your temper. Imagine your temper as a puppy inside you that needs some training. The puppy is not bad — it will probably turn out to be a great dog. It just needs to learn some rules because, right now, that puppy is causing some problems for you.

You don't want to keep getting in trouble for the way you act when you're angry. You probably even feel bad afterward if you've hurt someone's feelings or broken a toy you liked. So let's get that puppy trained.

Here are steps to take anytime, even when you're not angry:

- **Get lots of physical activity.** Play outside. Do sports you like. Karate or wrestling can be good for kids who are trying to get their tempers under control. But any activity that gets your heart pumping can be good because it's a way of burning off energy and stress. It feels good to boot that soccer ball or smack that baseball!
- **Talk to your mom or dad.** If you're having trouble with your temper, the time to talk about it is before you have another angry outburst. Tell your parents that you're trying to do a better job of controlling yourself. Ask for their help and ideas for how you could do this better. Maybe if you go a whole week without a meltdown, they can take you out for a treat. Let them know that if you do get really angry, you're going to ask for their help.
- **Put feelings into words.** Get in the habit of <u>saying what you're feeling</u> and why. Tell your parents, "I feel angry when you tell me it's time to stop playing and take out the trash. I don't like taking out the trash." And your parent will probably say (kindly), "I know — no one likes doing it. But it's your job, and you need to do it anyway." So using words won't get you out of taking out the trash (sorry!), but it might stop you from slamming the garage door, having a fit about the trash, or doing something else that could get you in trouble. Using words helps people manage their strong feelings and behaviors.
- **Take control.** Who's in charge here — you or that wild little puppy? Decide that you're going to be in charge. Don't let those angry feelings make you do stuff you don't want to do.

The real test comes the next time you get so mad you could just explode. But don't explode. Put a leash on that puppy with these four steps:

1. **Take a break from the situation.** If you're in an argument with someone, go to another part of your house. Your room or the backyard are good choices. Just say, "I want to be alone for a while so I can calm down."
2. **Put yourself in a timeout.** If you're feeling angry and think you need a timeout to calm down, don't wait for a parent to tell you — go ahead and take a timeout for yourself. Let your family know that when you're taking a timeout, they need to respect your space and leave you alone to calm yourself down. For kids old enough to do it for themselves, a timeout isn't a punishment: It's a cool-down. While you're sitting in your timeout chair, try this cool-down exercise: Put your hands under the seat of the chair and pull up while you count to five. Then stretch your arms over your head. Take a nice deep breath and let it out. One kid who tried these steps said he used this time to think about the consequences — like getting in trouble if he let his temper go wild.
3. **Get the anger out.** We don't want you punching walls (or even punching pillows), but why not do a bunch of jumping jacks or dance around your room to your favorite music? Turn it up a little. If you go outside, run around or do cartwheels across the lawn. You also could pick up your pen and write it all down. What made you so upset? Keep writing until you've covered everything. If you don't like writing, just draw a picture that

helps you express your feelings. Use strong colors and strong lines to show your strong feelings. You also can try the "Be a Volcano" exercise.

4. **Learn to shift.** You'll have to work hard to do this. This is where you get that puppy under control. The idea is to shift from a really angry mood to a more in-control mood. After you get some of the angry feelings out, you have to start thinking about other things. Sometimes, when people are angry, they're not really thinking clearly. They're just mad, mad, mad. Only angry thoughts are flying around their brains. A person might even say mean things to himself or herself, like "I'm such an idiot. I lost my temper again!" But you can replace those thoughts with better ones. For instance, you can say, "I lost my temper, but I'm going to get myself under control now." Instead of thinking of the person or situation you're angry with, think of something else. Think of something that will put you in a better mood.

A Tough Question

What if it's a problem that can't be solved? Like being angry about your parents' <u>divorce</u>, or having to go to summer school, or wanting a later bedtime? Or when you just can't get your way about something? Some stuff kids get angry about can't be changed. For instance, if your mom says it's time to stop playing your videogame and go to bed, what can you do? She's not changing her mind, and you have to get some sleep. Man, that really stinks! You were almost to level four!

But even if you get really angry, she won't budge. And even if you knock over a chair, you'll still have to stop playing your game. But now you might have an extra penalty for knocking over the chair. Maybe she'll say you aren't allowed to play your game tomorrow! That would be very bad news — you'd have to wait even longer to get to level four.

Though it's one of the toughest things to learn, it might be best just to tell yourself, "OK, stop the game and get to bed." Some arguments you'll be able to win, but this probably isn't one of them.

That doesn't mean you'll never get your way. You **will** be able to get your way sometimes. Bigger kids, like you, can learn to make their points calmly without losing it. This approach usually works better with everyone, especially parents. When you do this, you're controlling that wild little puppy inside you. You're in charge instead of that little rascal with the wagging tail.

Have you been wondering why we asked you to think of your temper as a puppy? A puppy is young and loveable — just like you — and wonderful to be around, especially when it keeps its temper under control!

Reviewed by: D'Arcy Lyness, PhD
Date reviewed: October 2008

Cyberbullying

Surviving Cyberbullying

Leigh was in eighth grade when the messages started — first, a weird text on her new cell phone, then some angry-sounding IMs. Her first year in high school, she learned that some of her classmates had created a website specifically to upset her. The emails, texts, and MySpace posts got worse. It was so bad that she eventually changed schools.

Now eighteen, Leigh says she has come through the experience more self-aware and compassionate toward others. It was a terrible time, she says, but with some counseling and support from adults and friends, she was able to make sense of what happened to her.

Nearly half of all teens have been the victims of what has come to be called "cyberbullying." According to several recent studies, it's a problem that is on the rise. The good news is that our awareness of cyberbullying and what works to prevent it is growing even faster.

Here are some suggestions on what to do if you, or someone you know, is involved with online bullying.

What Counts as Cyberbullying?

Cyberbullying is the use of technology to harass, threaten, embarrass, or target another person. Online threats or "flames" (rude texts, IMs, or messages) count. So does posting personal information or videos designed to hurt or embarrass someone else.

Online bullying can be easier to commit than other acts of bullying because the bully doesn't have to confront the victim in person. Some cyberbullies probably don't realize just how hurtful their actions are.

By definition, cyberbullying involves young people. If an adult sends the messages or notes, it may meet the legal definition of cyber-harassment or cyber-stalking.

Virtual Acts, Real Consequences

Because of the role technology plays in our lives, there is often no place to hide from bullies. Online bullying can happen at home as well as school (even in the coffee shop or anywhere else people go online). And it can happen twenty-four hours a day.

Sometimes, online bullying, like other kinds of bullying, can leave people at risk for serious problems: Stress from being in a constant state of upset or fear can lead to problems with mood, energy level, sleep, and appetite. It can also make someone feel jumpy, anxious, or sad.

It's not just the person being bullied who gets hurt — the punishment for cyberbullies can be serious. More and more schools and after-school programs are creating systems to respond to cyberbullying. Schools may kick bullies off sports teams or suspend them from school. Some types of cyberbullying may violate school codes or even break antidiscrimination or sexual harassment laws, so a bully may face serious legal trouble.

Why Do People Do It?

Why would someone be a cyberbully? There are probably as many reasons as there are <u>bullies</u> themselves.

Sometimes, what seems like cyberbullying may be accidental. The impersonal nature of text messages, IMs, and emails makes it very hard to detect a sender's tone, and one person's joke could be another's devastating insult.

Most people know when they're being bullied, though, as bullying involves relentless teasing or threats. The people doing the bullying know they've crossed a line, too. It's not a one-off joke or insult — it's constant harassment and threats.

Intentional online bullying can be a sign that the bully is feeling hurt, frustrated, or angry, and is lashing out at others.

What to Do

If you're being bullied, harassed, or teased in a hurtful way — or know someone who is — there is no reason to suffer in silence. In fact, you absolutely should report upsetting IMs, emails, texts, etc.

Tell someone. Most experts agree: the first thing to do is tell an adult you trust. This is often easier said than done. Teens who are cyberbullied may feel embarrassed or reluctant to report a bully. But bullying can escalate, so speak up until you find someone to help.

Most parents are so concerned about protecting their kids that sometimes they focus on taking all precautions to stop the bullying. If you're being bullied and worry about losing your Internet or phone privileges, explain your fears to your parents. Let them know how important it is to stay connected, and work with them to figure out a solution that doesn't leave you feeling punished as well. You may have to do some negotiating on safe cell phone or computer use — the most important thing is to first get the bullying under control.

You can also talk to your school counselor or trusted teacher or other family member. If the bullying feels like it's grinding your life down, counseling can help. If you're not ready for that, you can still benefit from the support of a trusted adult.

Walk away. That tip you've heard about walking away from a real-life bully works in the virtual world, too. Knowing that you can step away from the computer (or turn off your phone) allows you to keep things in perspective and focus on the good things in your life. Ignoring bullies is the best way to take away their power. Sometimes ignoring a bully isn't easy to do — just try the best you can.

Report it to your service provider. Sites like Facebook, MySpace, or YouTube take it seriously when people use their sites to post cruel or mean stuff or set up fake accounts. If users report abuse, the site administrator may block the bully from using the site in future. You can also complain to phone service or email providers (such as Gmail, Verizon, Comcast, and Yahoo) if someone is bothering you.

Block the bully. Most devices have settings that allow you to electronically block the bully or bullies from sending notes. If you don't know how to do this, ask a friend or adult who does.

Don't respond. Resist the urge to "fight back." In some cases, standing up to a bully can be effective, but it's also more likely to provoke the person and escalate the situation. Ask an adult to intervene instead — after all, fighting fire with fire just leaves everything burned.

Although it's not a good idea to respond to a bully, it is a good idea to save evidence of the bullying if you can. It can help you prove your case, if needed. You don't have to keep mean emails, texts, or other communications where you see them all the time — you can forward them to a parent or save them to a flash drive.

Be safe online. Password protect your cell phone and your online sites, and change your passwords often. Be sure to share your passwords only with your parent or guardian. It's also wise to think twice before sharing personal information or photos/videos that you don't want the world to see. Once you've posted a photo or message, it can be difficult or impossible to delete. So remind yourself to be cautious when posting photos or responding to someone's upsetting message.

If a Friend Is a Bully

If you see a friend acting as a cyberbully, take him or her aside and gently talk about it. Perhaps there's a reason behind the bullying, and you can help your friend think about what it is. Or, if you don't know the person well enough to talk about feelings, just stand up for your own principles: Let the bully know it's not cool. Explain that it can have very serious consequences for the bully as well as "bystanders" like you and your friends who may feel stressed out or upset about what's going on.

Reviewed by: Michelle New, PhD
December 2008
©1995- 2010 . *The Nemours Foundation/KidsHealth®. Reprinted with permission.*

About Teen Suicide

When a teen commits suicide, everyone is affected. Family members, friends, teammates, neighbors, and sometimes even those who didn't know the teen well might experience feelings of grief, confusion, guilt — and the sense that if only they had done something differently, the suicide could have been prevented.

So it's important to understand the forces that can lead teens to suicide and to know how to help.

About Teen Suicide

The reasons behind a teen's suicide or attempted suicide can be complex. Although suicide is relatively rare among children, the rate of suicides and suicide attempts increases tremendously during adolescence. Suicide is the third -leading cause of death for fifteen to twenty-four-year-olds, according to the Centers for Disease Control and Prevention (CDC), surpassed only by accidents and homicide.

The risk of suicide increases dramatically when kids and teens have access to <u>firearms</u> at home, and nearly sixty percent of all suicides in the United States are committed with a gun. That's why any gun in your home should be unloaded, locked, and kept out of the reach of children and teens. Ammunition should be stored and locked apart from the gun, and the keys for both should be kept in a different area from where you store your household keys. Always keep the keys to any firearms out of the reach of children and adolescents.

Suicide rates differ between boys and girls. Girls think about and attempt suicide about twice as often as boys, and tend to attempt suicide by overdosing on drugs or cutting themselves. Yet boys die by suicide about four times as often girls, perhaps because they tend to use more lethal methods, such as firearms, hanging, or jumping from heights.

Which Kids Are at Risk for Suicide?

It can be hard to remember how it felt to be a teen, caught in that gray area between childhood and adulthood. Sure, it's a time of tremendous possibility but it can also be a period of great confusion and anxiety. There's pressure to fit in socially, to perform academically, and to act responsibly. There's the awakening of sexual feelings, a growing self-identity, and a need for autonomy that often conflicts with the rules and expectations set by others.

A teen with an adequate support network of friends, family, religious affiliations, peer groups, or extracurricular activities may have an outlet to deal with everyday frustrations. But many teens don't believe they have that, and feel disconnected and isolated from family and friends. These teens are at increased risk for suicide.

Factors that increase the risk of suicide among teens include:

- a psychological disorder, especially <u>depression</u>, bipolar disorder, and <u>alcohol</u> and <u>drug use</u> (in fact, approximately ninety-five percent of people who die by suicide have a psychological disorder at the time of death)
- feelings of distress, irritability, or agitation
- feelings of hopelessness and worthlessness that often accompany depression (a teen, for example, who experiences repeated failures at school, who is overwhelmed by violence at home, or who is isolated from peers is likely to experience such feelings)
- a previous suicide attempt
- a family history of depression or suicide (depressive illnesses may have a genetic component, so some teens may be predisposed to suffer major depression)
- physical or sexual abuse
- lack of a support network, poor relationships with parents or peers, and feelings of social isolation
- dealing with homosexuality in an unsupportive family or community, or hostile school environment

Warning Signs

Suicide among teens often occurs following a stressful life event, such as a perceived failure at school, a breakup with a boyfriend or girlfriend, the death of a loved one, a divorce, or a major family conflict.

A teen who is thinking about suicide might:

- talk about suicide or death in general
- talk about "going away"
- talk about feeling hopeless or feeling guilty

- pull away from friends or family
- lose the desire to take part in favorite things or activities
- have trouble concentrating or thinking clearly
- experience changes in eating or sleeping habits
- self-destructive behavior (drinking alcohol, taking drugs, or driving too fast, for example)

What Can Parents Do?

Most teens who commit or attempt suicide have given some type of warning to loved ones ahead of time. So it's important for parents to know the warning signs so that kids who might be suicidal can get the help they need.

Watch and Listen

Keep a close eye on a teen that seems depressed and withdrawn. Poor grades, for example, may signal that your teen is withdrawing at school.

It's important to keep the lines of communication open and express your concern, support, and love. If your teen confides in you, show that you take those concerns seriously. A fight with a friend might not seem like a big deal to you in the larger scheme of things, but for a teen it can feel immense and consuming. It's important not to minimize or discount what your teen is going through, as this can increase his or her sense of hopelessness.

If your teen doesn't feel comfortable talking with you, suggest a more neutral person, such as another relative, a clergy member, a coach, a school counselor, or your child's doctor.

Ask Questions

Some parents are reluctant to ask teens if they have been thinking about suicide or hurting themselves. Some fear that by asking, they will plant the idea of suicide in their teen's head.

It's always a good idea to ask, even though doing so can be difficult. Sometimes it helps to explain why you're asking. For instance, you might say: "I've noticed that you've been talking a lot about wanting to be dead. Have you been having thoughts about trying to kill yourself?"

Get Help

If you learn that your child is thinking about suicide, get help immediately. Your doctor can refer you to a psychologist or psychiatrist, or your local hospital's department of psychiatry can provide a list of doctors in your area. Your local mental health association or county medical society can also provide references. In an emergency, you can call **(800) SUICIDE** or **(800) 999-9999**.

If your teen is in a crisis situation, your local emergency room can conduct a comprehensive psychiatric evaluation and refer you to the appropriate resources. If you're unsure about whether you should bring your child to the emergency room, contact your doctor or call (800) SUICIDE for help.

If you've scheduled an appointment with a mental health professional, make sure to keep the appointment, even if your teen says he or she is feeling better. Suicidal thoughts do tend to come and go; however, it is important that your teen get help developing the skills necessary to decrease the likelihood that suicidal thoughts and behaviors will emerge again if a crisis arises.

If your teen refuses to go to the appointment, discuss this with the mental health professional — and consider attending the session and working with the clinician to make sure your teen has access to the help needed. The clinician might also be able to help you devise strategies to help your teen want to get help.

Remember that any ongoing conflicts between a parent and child can fuel the fire for a teen who is feeling isolated, misunderstood, devalued, or suicidal. Get help to air family problems and resolve them in a constructive way. Also let the mental health professional know if there is a history of depression, substance abuse, family violence, or other stresses at home, such as an ongoing environment of criticism.

Helping Teens Cope With Loss

What should you do if someone your teen knows, perhaps a friend or a classmate, has attempted or committed suicide? First, acknowledge your child's many emotions. Some teens say they feel guilty — especially those who felt they could have interpreted their friend's actions and words better.

Others say they feel angry with the person who committed or attempted suicide for having done something so selfish. Still others say they feel no strong emotions. All of these reactions are appropriate; emphasize to your teen that there is no right or wrong way to feel.

When someone attempts suicide and survives, people may be afraid of or uncomfortable about talking with him or her about it. Tell your teen to resist this urge; this is a time when a person absolutely needs to feel connected to others.

Many schools address a student's suicide by calling in special counselors to talk with the students and help them cope. If your teen is dealing with a friend or classmate's suicide, encourage him or her to make use of these resources or to talk to you or another trusted adult.

If You've Lost a Child to Suicide

For parents, the death of a child is among the most painful losses imaginable. For parents who've lost a child to suicide, the pain and grief may be intensified. Although these feelings may never completely go away, survivors of suicide can take steps to begin the healing process:

- Maintain contact with others. Suicide can be a very isolating experience for surviving family members because friends often don't know what to say or how to help. Seek out supportive people to talk with about your child and your feelings. If those around you seem uncomfortable about reaching out, initiate the conversation and ask for their help.
- Remember that your other family members are grieving, too, and that everyone expresses grief in their own way. Your other children, in particular, may try to deal with their pain alone so as not to burden you with additional worries. Be there for each other through the tears, anger, and silences — and, if necessary, seek help and support together.
- Expect that anniversaries, birthdays, and holidays may be difficult. Important days and holidays often reawaken a sense of loss and anxiety. On those days, do what's best for your emotional needs, whether that means surrounding yourself with family and friends or planning a quiet day of reflection.
- Understand that it's normal to feel guilty and to question how this could have happened, but it's also important to realize that you might never get the answers you seek. The healing that takes place over time comes from reaching a point of forgiveness — for both your child and yourself.
- Counseling and support groups can play a tremendous role in helping you to realize you are not alone.

Reviewed by: Matthew K. Nock, PhD
Date reviewed: June 2008
1995- 2010 . The Nemours Foundation/KidsHealth®. Reprinted with permission.

INFORMATION AND EMPOWERMENT RESOURCES FOR PARENTS AND TEACHERS

COMMUNICATING THE MESSAGE
OF NON-VIOLENCE

- **Develop open communication**

  It is important that you talk with children openly and honestly. Use encouragement, support, and positive reinforcement so your children know that they can ask any question on any topic freely and without fear of consequence. Provide straightforward answers; otherwise, your child may make up his or her own explanations that can be more frightening than any honest response you could offer. If you don't know the answer, admit it and then find the correct information and explore it together. Use everyday opportunities to talk as occasions for discussion. Some of the best talks you'll have with your child will take place when you least expect them. Remember that it often takes more than a single talk for children to grasp all they need to know, so talk, talk, and talk again.

- **Encourage children and young adults to talk things out**

  Children feel better when they talk about their feelings. It lifts the burden of having to face their fears alone and offers an emotional release. If you sense that a violent event (whether real or fictional) has upset your child, you might say something like, "That TV program we saw seemed pretty scary to me. What did you think about it?" and see where the conversation leads. If your child appears to constantly feel depressed, angry, or persecuted, it is especially important to reassure the child that you love him or her and encourage talking about his or her concerns. And if the child has been violent or a victim of violence, it is critical to give him or her a safe place to express feelings.

- **Monitor the media**

  Over the years, many experts have concluded that viewing a lot of violence in the media can be risky for children. Studies have shown that watching too much violence whether on TV, in the movies, or in video games can increase the chance that children will be desensitized to violence or even act more aggressively themselves. Pay special attention to the kinds of media your children play with or watch. Parental advisories for music, movies, TV, video, and computer games can help you choose age-appropriate media for your children. Try watching TV or playing video games with your children, and talk with them about the things you see together. Encourage your children to think about what they are watching, listening to, or playing, and ask how they would handle situations differently? Let them know why violent movies or games disturb you. For example, you might tell your nine-year-old, "Violence just isn't funny to me. In real life, people who get shot have families and children, and it's sad when something bad happens to them." Watching the news and other media with your child enables you to discuss current events.

- **Parents and other caring adults can help tone down the effects of these violent messages.**
  - Actively supervise your child's exposure to all forms of media violence.
  - Limit TV viewing to those programs you feel are appropriate.
  - Be selective about which movies your child sees and which video and computer games he or she plays.

• Establish rules about the Internet by going on-line together to choose sites that are appropriate and fun for your child.
• Consider using monitoring tools for TV and the Internet such as the v-chip, a new technology that allows parents to block TV programs they consider inappropriate.
• Take advantage of the ratings system that provides parents with information about the content of a TV program or movie.

- **Acknowledge your children's fears and reassure them of their safety**
  Children who experience or witness violence as well as those who have only seen violent acts on TV or in the movies often become anxious and fearful. That's why it's important to reassure a child that their personal world can remain safe. Try saying something like this to your seven- or eight-year-old: "I know that you are afraid. I will do my very best to make sure you are safe." The school tragedies in Colorado and in Georgia have shown that violence cannot only frighten children, but it can also make them feel guilty for not preventing it. By providing consistent support and an accepting environment, you can help reduce children's anxieties and fears.

- **Take a stand**
  Parents need to be clear and consistent about the values they want to instill. Don't cave in to your children's assertion that "everybody else does it" (or has seen it) when it comes to allowing them to play what you view as an excessively violent game or to watch an inappropriate movie. You have a right and responsibility to say, "I don't like the message that game sends. I know that you play that game at your friend's house, but I don't want it played in our house."

- **Control your own behavior**
  When it comes to learning how to behave, children often follow their parents' lead, which is why it is important to examine how you approach conflict. Do you use violence to settle arguments? When you're angry, do you yell or use physical force? If you want your child to avoid violence, model the right behavior for him or her.

- **Set limits regarding children's actions towards others**
  Let your child know that teasing can become bullying and roughhousing can get out of control. If you see your child strike another, impose a "time out" in order for the child to calm down, and then ask him or her to explain why he or she hit the other child. Firmly explain that hitting is not allowed and help the child figure out a peaceful way to settle the problem.

- **Hold family or class meetings**
  Regularly scheduled family or class meetings can provide an acceptable place to talk about complaints and share opinions. Just be sure that everyone gets a chance to speak. Use these meetings to demonstrate effective problem-solving and negotiation skills. Keep the meetings lively, but well controlled so children learn that conflicts can be settled without violence.

- **Convey strict rules about weapons**

  Teach your child that real guns and knives are very dangerous and that they can hurt and kill people. You might say, "I know in the cartoons you watch and the video and computer games you play, the characters are always shooting each other. They never get hurt; they just pop up again later like nothing ever happened. In real life, someone who gets shot will be seriously hurt; sometimes they even die."

- **Talk about gangs and cliques**

  Gangs and cliques are often a result of young people looking for support and belonging. However, they can become dangerous when acceptance depends upon negative or antisocial behavior. If you believe your child might be exposed or attracted to a gang, talk about it together. Look for an opportunity and say, "You know, sometimes it seems like joining a gang might be cool, but it's not. Children in gangs get hurt. Some even get killed because they try to solve their problems through violence. Really smart children choose friends who are fun to be with and won't put them in any danger." Many communities have programs that help prevent gang violence.

- **Talk with other parents**

  Help give your children a consistent anti-violence message by speaking with the parents of your children's friends about what your children can and cannot view or play in their homes. Ask other parents if there's a gun in their home. If there is, talk with them to make sure they've taken the necessary safety measures. Having this kind of conversation may seem uncomfortable, but keep in mind that nearly forty percent of accidental handgun shootings of children under sixteen occur in the homes of friends and relatives.

- **Pay particular attention to boys**

  Most boys love action, but action need not become violence. Parents must distinguish between the two and help their boys do so as well. Allow them safe and healthy outlets for their natural energy, and recognize that talking especially about violence is different for boys than for girls. Boys may feel ashamed to express their real feelings about violence. Instead of sitting down for a talk, initiate the topic while engaged in an activity he enjoys. Provide privacy for these conversations, and be ready to listen when he's ready to talk, even if the timing isn't ideal. (Pollack, Real Boys, 1998.)

- **Support and encourage a proactive policy against violence at school**

  Find out about your school's violence prevention efforts. Encourage the teaching of conflict resolution skills and peer mediation programs (where children counsel other children). Suggest training for de-escalating and preventing violence at school.

WHAT SHOULD YOU LOOK FOR WHEN DEALING WITH VIOLENCE?

THE STAGES OF FRUSTRATION

AND APPROPRIATE RESPONSES

1. **Anxiety:** Child sighs or uses other nonverbal cues. Teacher can respond by active listening and nonjudgmental talk.

2. **Stress:** Child exhibits minor behavior problems. Teacher can use proximity control, boost child interest, or provide assistance with assignments.

3. **Defensiveness:** Child argues and complains. Teacher can remind child of rules, use conflict resolution, and encourage child to ask for help.

4. **Physical Aggression:** Child has lost control and may hit, bite, kick, or throw objects. Teacher can escort the child from class, get help, restrain child if necessary, and protect the safety of the other children.

5. **Tension Reduction:** Child releases tension through crying or verbal venting or may become sullen and withdrawn. Teacher can decide whether to use supportive or punishment techniques (or both) and help the child gain insight into feelings and behavior.

AGGRESSIVE BEHAVIOR IS LEARNED AND MAINTAINED IN A MANNER SIMILAR TO OTHER BEHAVIORS.

Three important factors in behavior development and modification are modeling, positive reinforcement, and negative reinforcement.

Teachers and peers may be modeling inappropriate or aggressive behavior without being aware of its undue influence on an aggressive child. Similarly, they may reinforce disruptive behaviors either positively (through attention to the child) or negatively (through the removal of the child from class or similar constraint which allows him or her to escape or avoid what is perceived to be an aversive situation).

Aggressive children often exhibit deficits in social information processing; they are likely to misinterpret social cues and wrongly direct hostile intent to others, especially during times of stress. They are more likely than others to have some social skills deficits such as poor impulse control, low frustration tolerance, limited ability to generate alternative responses to stress, and limited insight into the feelings of self and others.

PREVENTION AND INTERVENTION

Prevention and intervention at an early age have afforded the most positive results in changing the outcome of a child's future and level of violence. It has even proven to be the most cost-effective manner in which to deal with violence.

> **prevention** – child chooses not to engage in violent acts

> **intervention** – when child engages in or perpetrates aggressive or violent acts, he or she is stopped and redirected into non-violent problem solving.

Non-violence must be modeled and reinforced—acknowledging behavior through consequences or acts that are unpleasant is often necessary; however, certain punishments can be view by children as acts of violence. Even consequences should be tailored to promote non-violence (i.e. exclusion from the group versus spanking).

There is no gene for violence. Violence is a learned behavior, and it is often learned at home and from family members, friends, or media. Children are more aggressive and grow up more likely to become involved in violence—either as victims or victimizers—if they witness violent acts. A 1994 report by the APA Commission on Violence and Youth shows it is possible to predict a child who will be prone to violence by observing their level of aggression at an early age.

Unfortunately, this study also showed that the violence in these young people eventually ended in criminal behaviors.

EIGHT NEEDS OF ALL CHILDREN

1. Love and support from peers and people with whom they interact

2. Empowerment through feeling valuable and safe

3. Understanding of the boundaries and expectations of others

4. A strong sense of identity, knowing and respecting who they are as individuals and as they relate to others

5. Positive values and specific morals to help guide their decisions and choices

6. Positive peer and family relationships that they help to build

7. Freedom from fear of failure and degradation

8. Commitment to other people, goals, and situations and commitment from others.

LOVE AND SAFETY ARE BASIC NEEDS FOR EVERYBODY

ABRAHAM MASLOW'S HIERACHY OF NEEDS

The need for
self-
actualisation

Experience purpose,
meaning and realising
all inner potentials.

Esteem Need
The need to be a unique individual with
self-respect and to enjoy general
esteem from others.

Love and belonging needs
The need for belonging, to receive and give love,
appreciation, friendship.

Security Need
The basic need for social security in a family and a society
that protects against hunger and violence.

The physiological needs
The need for food, water, shelter and clothing

Child's Hierarchy of Needs

© PhD in Parenting Blog 2009
www.phdinparenting.com

Self-actualization

Hobbies, languages, creative pursuits

Esteem

Encouragement, protection from bullying and discrimination, respect from parents/teachers/peers, positive discipline, learning life skills

Social Needs

Unconditional love, loving interaction with caregivers, room to explore and play, interaction with peers

Safety and Security

Adult caregivers to protect from danger (car seats, babyproofing, watchful eye), plan if something happens to parents, being above poverty line, access to health care, free from abuse or neglect.

Physiological

Healthy (age appropriate) food, sleep, shelter, human touch

BASIC LESSON PLANS FOR SELECTED H.U.Y.O.E. TOPICS AND WORKSHEETS

LESSON PLAN FOR "CARING IS SHARING"

GOAL:

The goal of this lesson is that every child participates in group discussions by volunteering information or by responding to verbal or written questions, and that positive reinforcement will be the result of positive participation.

MATERIALS: All worksheets on "Caring and Sharing"

The "I Shared. I Cared." Award

Crayons or markers

OBJECTIVES:

1.   The *H.U.Y.O.E. Non-Violence Guide for Children* will be introduced to groups with the expectation that all children will be expected to actively participate.

2.   The children will give their own definitions of "sharing" and examples of how they can share with their minds and voices. (Be sure to repeat and elaborate on all appropriate answers while making positive suggestions for the less appropriate answers.)

3.   The children will give their own definition of "caring" as well as examples of how they show that they care for themselves and how they care for other people. (Be sure to repeat and elaborate on all appropriate answers while making positive suggestions for the less appropriate answers.)

4.   Reasons why group discussions are important will be discussed with emphasis on the understanding that discussion helps children who may be afraid to speak out loud and gives children a chance to learn the thoughts and personalities of others. Modeling good conversation strategies and techniques is crucial to this lesson.

As each child gives an answer, give them an award. Explain that they will have a chance to earn additional awards during the future discussions. Encourage all of the child's family members to become a part of the positive reinforcement process.

EVALUATION:

Observations of each child's action and reaction to the topics regarding violence are crucial to every lesson. Since the topics are very specific to certain types of aggressive behavior, adults will have opportunities to hone in on the level of sensitivity that each child exhibits toward the different forms of aggression and violent behaviors. It will be helpful to note specific behavior, responses, and body language during any interchange between peers and adults.

While the children are talking and participating in the group discussion, the children should be allowed to interact with each other and should be encouraged to comment upon each others' responses. If a response is a negative response, the teacher should stop the discussion immediately and **model** a positive reaction or response to what has been said. Positive reinforcement can also be modeled commending children following appropriate answers and by having the children applaud each other after each child speaks, regardless how short the response.

A chart could be displayed showing the number of awards each child has earned over a period of time. Each child should be encouraged to speak and share during every class discussion.

Finally, the "I Shared. I Cared." Award should be given to every child who participated, regardless of how short the response or regardless of the quality of the responses. This is the time to encourage the children to simply participate in verbal discussions.

NOTES:

_____

_____

_____

_____

_____

_____

_____

FOLLOW UP:

_____

_____

_____

_____

LESSON PLAN FOR "THE STORY OF LIL V AND THE VCREW"

GOAL:

The teacher will read the story introducing LIL VMAN and the V-CREW aloud to the children, pausing for questions when necessary. Each child will understand that there are good influences and bad influences in the world that affect our behavior. The children will understand that if we work together to promote what is good and right, even if we don't understand all of the reasons, good choices can overcome the bad situations.

MATERIALS: The Story of Lil VMan and the V-Crew

All worksheets and posters of Lil VMan and the V-Crew

Chalkboard and chalk or Whiteboard and marker for "Big Words"

Drawing paper for responses (K-1)

Writing or notebook paper for responses (grades 2 – 6)

Pencils

Crayons, markers, colored pencils

OBJECTIVES:

1. Each child will listen to the entire story of Lil VMan and the V-Crew.
2. Each child will recognize the Lil V is the hero of the World of Kids.
3. Each child will recognize and name the members of the V-Crew.
4. Each child will be able to state, in their own words, what the **PROBLEM** is in the story.
5. **Re-read the text of the paragraph that begins with the words, "They formed an immediate…", emphasizing the words that are written in capital letters and bold print. These ten terms are "Big Words" that the children will learn to pronounce. Each child will pronounce each word correctly at least three times.**
6. The ten **"Big Words"** (highlighted terms) should be displayed on the board or on word cards. **Each child will write down at least three of these "Big Word" terms on word cards or notebook paper and take them home as a family homework project.**
7. **The children will recognize the resolution of the problem presented in this story** and be able to explain what happened to help resolve the problem.

EVALUATION:

1.   Each child will present their words to their family and writ the definition of each term with their family's help the definition for the term will be written. The child will share with the class what their words are and what the definitions of their terms are. Out of the three terms, each child will pronounce and define at least two of the words and terms correctly.

2.   Each child will be able to discuss what the solution was to keep the sky from falling.

3.   The teacher will explain that the "hidden" message is "We must all try to hold up our own part of the world."

4.   Each child will be able to explain this message in his or her own words.

GROUP DISCUSSION QUESTIONS

1. Who is the hero that lives in the World of Kids?
    a.   Answer: *Lil V*
2. Do you remember the name of the group that helped Lil V?
    a.   Answer: *V-Crew.*
3. What were the names of the V-Crew?
    Answer: *B-Girl, G-Man, and Shuk-V duck.*
4. In the story that is told, what was the problem that B-Girl discovered? Answer: *That the negative ones were planning to make the sky fall all over the world.*
5. Who did the animals choose as a good leader for them to help solve their problem? Answer: *Shuck-V Duck*
6. Why do you think the other animals chose him? *Answers may vary.*
7. What was the solution that Shuk-V demonstrated? Answer: *He held up his part of the sky.*
8. How did the other animals respond? Answer: *Although they did not understand, they followed their leader and held up the sky over them. Therefore, the sky never fell on any of them.*
9. What lesson does this teach us? *Answers will vary.*

NOTES:

_____

_____

_____

FOLLOW UP:

_____

_____

LESSON PLAN FOR "LIL VMAN'S PLEDGE AGAINST VIOLENCE"

GOAL: Each child will understand that violence is a choice, but it has negative consequences that often hurt people we love or hurt ourselves.

MATERIALS: All worksheets and posters of "Lil VMan's Pledge Against Violence"

OBJECTIVES:

1.   The class will look at the poster entitled "Lil VMan's Pledge Against Violence".
2.   The teacher will read each line of the pledge and ask the children its meaning.
3.   The teacher will open the discussion about whether violence is a good choice or a bad choice and then explain to the group that we are always given the opportunity to make good and bad choices.
4.   The teacher should **model** the act of making a good choice, giving examples of how she or he had to make personal choices and the good choice that was made. Compare that choice with what would have been a bad choice.
5.   The children will discuss how they were faced with a choice and give the decision of the choice they made. The group will discuss each child's example and discuss whether is probably led to aggression or non-aggression.

Please remember, there may be many "bad" choices, but not bad children. Children should understand that their choices have consequences, but they are not the choices they have made. They are people, and people can make a difference.

6.   It may be helpful to have the students role play each line of the "Lil VMan's Pledge Against Violence".
7.   Each child will be given the opportunity to make the pledge against violence, if desired.
8.   Each child will be given their own personal copy of the "Lil VMan's Pledge Against Violence" and asked to find a good place to put it. (Suggest that they place it on the refrigerator door, bathroom door, mirror in their room, etc. The object is to have it placed where they and other family members can see it very often.)

EVALUATION:

1.   The children will be able to repeat the pledge with the help of the teacher or parent with ninety percent accuracy.
2.   The goal is for at least ninety percent of all of the children to be able to repeat the complete pledge with one hundred percent accuracy without teacher prompting by the end of the curriculum.
3.   At least ninety percent of the children will have at least one family member who will assist their child to learn the pledge.

4.   Every child will be rewarded for repeating the "Lil VMan's Pledge Against Violence".

5.   A second reward will be given to the children who bring a note back to school with signatures indicating that their family was actively involved in reading and discussing the pledge.

POSITIVE REINFORCEMENT:

A positive reward chart with a list of the children's names can be placed in a high activity or highly visual location (for instance, on the door of the classroom or wall where children are asked to line up) so that the children will be able to view it often. Next to each child's name, there should be spaces where stars or stickers can be placed. The stars can be used for each child who completes his or her worksheet, and the special stickers can be placed on chart next to the child's name when they involve their family in their lessons.

LESSON PLAN FOR "THE TALE OF HONEY BIZZIE BEE"

GOAL: Each child will understand that there are good influences and bad influences in the world that affect our behavior. The children will learn that how we feel about ourselves is very important. They will learn that having good self-esteem affects our lives and the lives of everyone around us. The children will learn that we should try to help everyone feel good about themselves and respect the differences we see in other people.

MATERIALS: The story: "The Tale of Honey Bizzie Bee"

All corresponding worksheets

Chalkboard and chalk or whiteboard and marker for story phrases

Writing or notebook paper for responses (grades 2 – 6)

Pencils

Crayons, markers, colored pencils

OBJECTIVES:

1. Each child will listen to the entire story of Honey Bizzie Bee
2. Each child will show that they understand the personality of Honey Bizzie Bee as a helpful person by naming something that they do to help others.
3. Each child should name at least two positive characteristics about Honey Bizzie Bee, and tell why this makes her a helpful character.
4. The children will also recognize the fact that her body is disproportionate in size and shape by looking at a picture of her and discussing her body.
5. **Older students should learn the actual insect body parts of the honey bee.**
6. As a group, discuss the attitudes of Walter Wasp and Harry Hornet.
7. Each child will be able to name at least two negative behaviors that are being exhibited by Walter and Harry.
8. Each child will state, in their own words, what the **problem** is in the story.
9. Each child should discuss how they think Honey Bizzie Bee feels about what is being said about her.
   a. Discuss what it means to have good self-esteem.
   b. Discuss why it is important to feel good about who you are.
   c. Discuss why it is important to respect the differences we all have.
   d. Discuss the importance of respecting other people's challenges.
10. Discuss the resolution of the problem presented in this story and why this resolution is appropriate.
11. The word phrases in the story that are colored blue should be written on the board. Older students should choose at least one of these phrases, research them, and write a paragraph or report of the phrases regarding their meaning.

12. The research paragraphs or reports should be read and discussed by the class.

EVALUATION:

1. Each child will discuss their feelings of self-esteem and how people around them make them feel and why.

2. Each child will be able to discuss solutions to the times when their self-esteem is affected in a negative way. Positive solutions should be discussed.

3. The teacher will explain the concept "We must all try to hold up our own end."

4. Each child will be able to express value in who they are and be able to explain why they are important.

5. As each child discusses why they are important, the group should be led in celebrating each child by applauding. Each child should be encouraged to take a bow for being who they are.

NOTES:

_____

_____

_____

_____

_____

_____

FOLLOW UP:

_____

_____

_____

_____

BIBLIOGRAPHY

Ballare, Antonia and Lampros Angelique (1994), Behavior Smart, The Center for Applied Research in Education, West Nyack, New York

.Purdy, J. David, Little People, Big Choices (1991) Christian Publications, Camp Hill, Pennsylvania.

Roehlkepartain, Eugene C., Building Assets In Congregations, "A Practical Guide for Helping Youth Grow Up Healthy", (1998) , Search Institute, Minneapolis, MN.

Ernst, Ken, Games Students Play (And What To Do About Them), (1975), Celestial Arts Publishing, Millbrae, California.

Ruffalo, Richard and Mike Moretti, P.E.P. The Seven P's to Positively Enhance Performance, (1996), Hara Publications, Seattle, WA

Hall, Jeff, Division of Violence Prevention, National Center for Injury Prevention and Control, Center for Disease Control and Prevention, (2007)

Hall, Jeff, U.S. Department of Education and U.S. Department of Justice, (2007)

Ryan Biliski l KidsHealth.org, Manager, Partner & Media Relations, The Nemours Foundation Center for Children's Health Media, Wilmington, DE, (1995 – 2010.)

http://www.theteacherscorner.net/printable-worksheets/make-your-own/word-search/word-search.php

ABOUT THE AUTHORS

SURVIVORS OF YOUTH VIOLENCE

Sharon Saddler

Sharon is the survivor of handgun violence perpetuated by a young person. As a result of her experience, she has worked to improve educational programs and encourage non-violence nationwide. She received her Bachelor of Science Degree in Language Arts and Special Education from the University of Michigan and her Masters Degree in Special Education and Elementary Education from Alabama A&M University. In addition to thirty-four years of teaching experience, she is the creator and coordinator of Princeton City's The Home-School Program, and the G.E.E.R.C. Community Literacy After-School Program. She spent years working with Ohio State Institutes for Reading Instruction, served as an executive board member of Parent Teacher Organization, and as the coordinator of the parent involvement and empowerment programs through Ohio's State Department of Education. Her training background includes ASCD (formerly the Association for Supervision and Curriculum Development) and Search Institute Asset-Building for Youth. She is the organizer for Cincinnati-based Victory Over Violence Organization for Ohio and the International Campaign for Victory Over Violence. Sharon also spent eight years as a theraputic foster parent for abused children. Sharon is the recepient of the PROS Award from Princeton City School District, the Best in the Southwest Award, and exemplary status ratings from the Ohio State Department of Education for her educational programs. She was also named Who's Who Among Teachers of America.

Fred Vman Watson

Fred is the survivor of the trauma and tragedy of three bullets shot into his head. He was dubbed "Miracle Man" and "Vman" ('V' for victory) by the University of Michigan medical staff due to the fact that he beat the odds of a six percent chance of life and eighty-seven percent chance of being in a vegetative state. He still carries one of the bullets in his head and was left legally blind. Formerly a member of the music and journalism industries, Fred is now a well-informed and sought-after motivational speaker. He is the creator of "Victory Over Violence," a campaign to fight violence all over the world, and has promoted this campaign through various schools, colleges, universities, sports leagues, nationwide group discussions, weekly national telephone conferences, and weekly primetime television broadcasts, as well as through many foundations and associations. Internationally, he has founded the International Campaign for Victory Over Violence USA-Italy and linked to the humanitarian arm of the United Nations via UNIPAX. He is also the founder of Dads On Duty, and has instituted Atlanta's Victory Over Violence Month and Georgia's State Capitol Annual Service Providers Day for victims and survivors of violence. Fred is the recipient of the International Liberty Award, the Gandhi Foundation Award, and Secretary of State Service Awards.

Mr. Watson also honors and acknowledges Mr. Rich Ruffalo and Mr. Bobby Byrd for their life achievements, and for the encouragement they provided for this project and H.U.Y.O.E.